*In This Very Moment*

# In This Very Moment

A Simple Guide to
Zen Buddhism

*James Ishmael Ford*

Skinner House Books
Boston

Published by Skinner House Books. Skinner House Books is an
imprint of the Unitarian Universalist Association, a liberal religious
organization with more than 1,000 congregations in the U.S. and
Canada. 25 Beacon Street, Boston, MA 02108-2800.

Printed in Canada.

Cover design by Kathryn Sky-Peck.
Text design by Suzanne Morgan.

ISBN 1-55896-439-8

Library of Congress Cataloging-in-Publication Data
Ford, James Ishmael.
In this very moment : a simple guide to Zen Buddhism /
James Ishmael Ford.
p. cm.
Includes bibliographical references.
ISBN 1-55896-433-9 (alk. paper)
Zen Buddhism—Doctrines. I. Title: Simple guide to
Zen Buddhism. II. Title.
BQ9268.3 .F67 2002
294.3'927—dc21                        2002021156

10 9 8 7 6 5 4 3 2 1
05 04 03 02

The first edition of this book was originally published as *This Very
Moment: A Brief Introduction to Buddhism and Zen for Unitarian Universalists.*

*for*
*Jan Seymour-Ford*

# Contents

# Acknowledgments

Space does not allow me to acknowledge everyone, or even a large percentage, of those who have helped and guided me as I've written this book. Still, a few names absolutely must be mentioned.

My Zen practice traces back more than thirty years. At the very beginning Shunryu Suzuki and Mel Sojun Weitsman introduced me to the Buddha way. Jiyu Kennett ordained me as a priest, and Jim Wilson, also known as Tundra Wind, opened the koan way for me. Masao Abe showed me how scholarship and insight are not incompatible. Certainly at the heart of my training John Tarrant has proven my true friend and an astonishingly agile guide along the trackless way.

The Unitarian Universalist congregations in Sonoma County and San Jose, California; Mequon, Wisconsin; Chandler, Arizona; and Newton, Massachusetts, have given me critical but loving forums to explore the ways in which

Western liberal religion and Buddhism complement and challenge each other. I am ever grateful to the teachers and community of the Pacific Zen Institute, as well as to my students and companions within the Zen Community of Boston. They have shown me the depth, beauty, and mystery that unfolds within authentic Zen sanghas.

I have particular debts in the writing of this book that I want to acknowledge as well. My spouse and live-in editor, Jan Seymour-Ford, has more than once uncovered a clear sentence in my great rat-piles of words. And at Skinner House Books, I owe much to Marshall Hawkins and Brenda Wong at the beginning and Mary Benard at the end, as well as to Patricia Frevert throughout the long journey to publication.

My gratitude to all these named and unnamed friends, companions, and teachers.

# Introduction

He sat in front of me, silently sobbing.

We'd been sitting together, twenty or so of us, in a Zen retreat called *sesshin*—"to touch the heart/mind." And, now, four deep days into it, we all were touching that heart, that mind, which is the source of both our pain and our joy. I was a brand-new Zen teacher and the man sitting in front of me was an old friend.

This was an important moment. In many ways we were learning together. At this instant my friend had moved from the facile brilliance that normally marked our conversations, to something ancient and animal.

"James," he said. "I feel this terrible longing." He paused. "I feel parts of me are lost." He gasped and rubbed his eyes. "I have open sores where these parts are gone. Wounds. And I want to be healed." Again, a long silence passed before he whispered, "I feel my whole life has been lost, wandering aimlessly."

It was about eleven o'clock in the morning, and we'd already been sitting, meditating, for about seven hours. We were in the middle of the private interview called *dokusan*. *Dokusan* literally means "coming to the teacher." In the Zen traditions it is the time when a student brings her or his question to the teacher. At this moment in my life, after some thirty years of Zen training and hundreds of *sesshin*, years of sitting, and thousands of *dokusan*, now I found myself the teacher.

At the beginning of that interview, my old friend and I were discussing what counts most. When we really pay attention to our lives, all our longing, all our hurt, all our hope is revealed. Nothing is hidden. In fact there are no secrets, no hidden truths. When we stop the grand rush of our lives, just for a moment, it is all revealed. It is not until we pay attention to this pain and longing within us that we can begin to walk an authentic spiritual path.

As we embark on the great way, we find ourselves confronted with suffering, both our own and that of those whom we love. When we confront this suffering honestly and humbly, it breaks our hearts. There is a profound sadness in our realizations as we examine ourselves and the world we live in.

But there is also good news here. Discovering our brokenness, sometimes we find ourselves pulled further along in our quest for meaning and purpose. Certainly, this was the journey my friend now found himself on. And it is the journey I've been on. It is the way the Buddha himself walked so many years before. It is the great way of Zen.

This slender book contains the fruit of my own journey of longing, of brokenness, of exploration, of finding. It is about what brought me to sit in that small room, facing a student with so much hurt and so much hope.

*Dividing the World*

There is an ancient Chinese folk story that speaks to the deep desire for knowing who we are, for reconciliation and healing, and how this quest might look. Its origin is lost in the mists of time, but nonetheless it speaks to this calling of our hearts so clearly that for nearly a thousand years it has been considered a Zen koan, an object for our deepest reflection. In one of the great anthologies of koan, the *Wu-men kuan*, the "Gateless Barrier," it has been included as the thirty-fifth case, "Which is the True Ch'ien?"

This story turns on two children raised together, Ch'ien and Chau. They were cousins being raised by Ch'ien's father, Chau's uncle. They were constant companions throughout their childhood. Ch'ien's father, Kien, one day said to them, "You two are perfect together. When you grow up, you will be married." The children let these words soak into them and decided it was true: they were betrothed to one another. Unlike most childish thoughts that fade away like a morning mist, they never wavered from their assumption that someday they would marry.

Of course, life rarely goes as we expect, and as they grew into young adulthood, as was the custom of that ancient culture Chang-kien arranged for Ch'ien to be married to a wealthy merchant. The young couple was devastated. Chau decided he couldn't bear to see his beloved Ch'ien wedded to someone else. He decided to leave home forever one night about a week before the wedding. He acquired a boat, and when that night came, he set off down river without a word to anyone.

He wasn't gone more than three or four minutes when he heard Ch'ien calling to him. Looking into the gloom, he saw her running down the bank of the river, her skirts rippling in the evening breeze. He pulled over, she climbed into the boat and they sailed away together.

They married and settled together in the province of Chuh. After six happy years and the birth of two children, Ch'ien said to her husband, "I have to go home and make peace with my father." Chau understood, feeling many of the same longings as his beloved, and agreed. So they arranged for the care of their children with friends and sailed back upstream to their old home.

When they moored, Ch'ien stayed in the boat while Chau went up to the house to ascertain what their reception would be. He knocked on the door and Kien answered it. "Oh, how wonderful to see you!" the old man exclaimed. "I've worried for years about you and what has happened to you." In violation of all cultural standards, he embraced the young man as if his lost son had returned home.

Chau was embarrassed, and replied, "Thank you, sir. I've missed you, too. But I really didn't expect such a greeting."

"Why not?" Kien asked. "I raised you as a son. I've missed you more than I can say."

"But, since I ran away with Ch'ien, I thought you would be terribly angry."

The old man stepped back and stared at his nephew. "What are you talking about? Ch'ien is here. The night you left she went to bed and has been in a coma ever since. Of course there never was a wedding. I've often thought that I should have let you two marry instead. Come." The two went into the house and, sure enough, in a darkened bedroom, there was Ch'ien, terribly pale, and obviously in a feverish sleep.

"I don't know what to say. But I have to show you something," Chau said to his uncle. Together the two men walked down toward the river. They were about halfway there when Ch'ien appeared. She was flushed and walking fast. She seemed not to see the two men at all, but instead was looking at something behind them. They turned to see the other Ch'ien, fevered and pale as silk, also walking rapidly toward the river. Frightened, Chau and Kien stood aside as the two Ch'iens ran up to each other, embraced and melted into one another, somehow becoming one person.

The great eleventh-century Zen master Wu-tsu Fa-yen took this traditional story and turned it into a koan, that object for meditation and conversation between Zen practitioners. Wu-tsu asked, "The woman Ch'ien and her spirit separated. Which is the true Ch'ien?"

Perhaps this is the question for all of us. It doesn't matter whether the question was formulated in the eleventh century or yesterday: it is a question about and for all of us: for my friend weeping for his home, for Ch'ien seeking her true self, for you and me as we engage the great questions of life and death, hope and longing. Here we ask, "Who are we? Who am I? What is my true self? What is my true home? And how do I find it?"

When I think about our lives today at the dawn of the third millennium of our Western culture, I find that this conversation is always beckoning. In the spiritual tradition I've found to be so important to me, we frequently find these burning questions presented as koan. A koan is a question about ultimate things that also holds the answer. In my friend's call, I feel that we find one of the most basic and important questions. At such a moment, we also find ourselves having come a long way toward its understanding.

Here I found my friend and student asking those same old questions for himself: How do we reconcile the broken heart? How do we find our way home?

Who is the true Ch'ien?

Who am I?

As these questions tumble out of us, all our ancient longings are revealed. Each facet of the question presents itself as a memory or a hope: the touch of a loved one, joy in making love, burning anger at a cutting word or unkind act, our desire for a better world. Like the many facets of a jewel, these hurts and joys combine to make up our lives, and indeed, life on this planet.

So, we might ask, what is it that splits into all these things? Here, perhaps, the question really is "What is the source of this joy and this sorrow that is so terrible and so compelling?" For many, this question boils down to: "Who am I?" Everything else echoes from that question: "Where am I going?" "Why do I die?" "What is the meaning of my life?" This is our call to know our true home, our true place.

This core question and all its reverberations are embedded somewhere deep within us. Once an individual emerges out of the great mystery, questions of identity and purpose and direction spill out in a great torrent. Naturally, we find this core question right at the beginning of our great Western collection of sacred stories, the Bible. In many ways the story of the Garden of Eden tells us about that home we all dream of and long for deep down. Within our bones and marrow and blood, we understand the story of that home, that place of purpose and meaning, of reconciliation and healing – that Garden – and we constantly dream of it.

This story from the Hebrew Bible tells us a lot about ourselves and about our original nature. It hints at what that home is like. It tells us something about how we've strayed from it. And, at least implicitly, it suggests how we can return.

At its heart, the action of the Biblical story of the Garden turns on human beings eating the fruit of the knowledge of good and evil. Worrying about who is responsible—the woman, the man, the serpent, or God—is to miss the lesson. Somehow it happened. And however it came about, when human beings first discerned that the primordial world can be divided, we did, indeed, become as gods.

This astonishing ability to divide the world, to separate you and me, to assign good and evil to actions—surely this is godlike. As we distinguish ourselves from nature, we discover astonishing powers. From this ability all our unique human behaviors are derived. Here we discover how to farm. Here we discover how to make a bow and an arrow. Here we discover how to build homes. Here we discover how to construct spaceships and nuclear bombs. We really have learned how to create good and evil.

But somehow this very ability has cast us out of the Garden. Ever since human beings first divided the world, we've felt lost, and we've longed for our true home. This is a common human experience. The question becomes: How do we deal with it? Are we doomed to the struggle? Or, is there a way back? And if so, how do we return to our home?

The truth isn't simple. There is no return to the womb. There is no return to unconsciousness. We've come too far. We've eaten of the fruit and have become as gods. And because of that, it is a whole new ball game. So the question becomes: How do we return home without sacrificing our full humanity? This is the hard task. How do we return to Eden as fully human beings?

Sometimes we have to wander far from home in order to really understand what home is. In my own case, as it was for my friend and student as well as for so many others, I had to wander far from the spiritualities of the West in order to understand the truths contained in my childhood stories. I've also been enriched, learning that my real home was never as narrow or constrained as I once thought it must be. So I believe all the wandering was worth it.

This book recounts some of that journey beyond east and west and toward our true home. It also, I hope, shows each of us, wherever we may be on the path, some of the signposts that can guide us through the trackless waste to our own Garden.

## Zen Comes West

It is important to briefly chart the path of Zen from its Asian origins to its broad and powerful expression in today's West. My own experience, marked as it is by so many different traditions, is in some ways an example of how Zen itself is heir to so much. Zen brings these things together, distills them, and presents the gold of wisdom. While it is a true child of its Eastern parentage, Zen has taken on new dimensions as it has traveled West, adding disciplines that have enriched the possibilities for Western teachers. To fully appreciate and use those riches, it is very important to try to understand these perspectives.

History really is prologue to the future. And in our consumer culture with its tendencies to pick and choose, we need to understand what it is we're choosing and what it is we're rejecting. The consequences of the choices we make now will play out for generations to come. Understanding the origins of the various forms of Buddhism we are now encountering frees us to see our current situation and to make choices that will allow this precious way to continue to heal many hearts.

It is impossible to say when Buddhism and Western culture met. In the nineteenth century, scholars discovered that the ancient Christian saints Barlaam and Josaphat were in fact the heroes of a retelling and Christianizing of the Buddha's story. The eighth-century Greek theologian St. John of Damascus published a widely reprinted account of these saints, but it was itself based on much older stories circulating for generations.

In the thirteenth century, the Franciscan friar William of Rubuck was sent on an embassy to the Mongol khan in quest of rumored Far Eastern Christians. He actually found some, the Nestorians, descendents of Christian missions from the early church. He also encountered Buddhists, and gave the first Western account of the Dharma. William's report is superficial, only describing what they looked like and producing a Latin transliteration of the Tibetan mantra *Om mani padme hum*. A few years later, writing about his own visit to the khan, Marco Polo gave the next Western—and this time slightly more accurate—accounting of Buddhism.

The mid-sixteenth-century Jesuit mission to Japan led by St. Francis Xavier records the next known encounters between Westerners and Zen. The Zen practitioners seemed to admire the Jesuits, and the Jesuit records show a certain begrudging respect for Zen adherents, as well. Here we find the first intimations of a potentially rich encounter, a hint that truly there are many mansions in heaven.

While most records from the Christian side of these early encounters are frankly polemical, with little regard for truth, an occasionally accurate account found its way into European languages. Englebert Kampfer's 1727 English language *History of Japan Together with a Description of the Kingdom of Sian* contains such a report. It includes an honest and even sympathetic description of the Obaku school of Zen.

The emerging Western enlightenment included an interest in Asian thought. The eighteenth-century scholar William Jones, friend of Benjamin Franklin and Joseph Priestly, the Unitarian minister and scientist, established an "Asiatick Society" that started translating Sanskrit texts, mainly Hindu, but also the beginnings of fragments of Buddhist literature. And Ceylonese and Tibetan Buddhism were at least described in the Society's journal.

Finally, the first actual Buddhist text appeared in English in 1844, in an issue of the American Unitarian Transcendentalist journal, the *Dial*. It was a chapter from the *Sadharmapundarika-sutra*, more commonly known today as the *Lotus Sutra*. It was actually a translation of an earlier French translation and was published anonymously. For years this seminal event was misattributed to Henry David Thoreau. However, "Anonymous" turns out to have been a woman, another prominent Transcendentalist and leader of New England Unitarianism, Elizabeth Palmer Peabody.

From this point the cat was out of the bag. Buddhism and Zen slowly began to attract the interest of intellectuals and scholars. Still, for the next hundred years, attention to Buddhism as a spiritual path mainly came from eccentrics. In the middle of the nineteenth century and well into the beginning of the twentieth, its widest reading in the West probably came through the work of the Russian adventuress and mystic Helena Petrova Blavatsky. Unfortunately, the teachings of her Theosophical Society made a hash of Buddhist doctrines. The consequences continue in our lives to this day.

Today scholars and other observers tend to focus on the question of "Orientalism," which might be understood as the misinterpretation of Asian religious traditions through imperialist and chauvinist lenses. "Theosophical Buddhism" is a grand example of how we can radically misunderstand a tradition if we are unclear about our own motives and assumptions.

On the other hand, Buddhism is itself an eclectic and dynamic tradition, always open to possibilities and new perspectives so long as they further the primary work: healing the broken heart, binding up the wounds, guiding us on our way toward our true home. The key, as in our spiritual disciplines, is to keep our eyes and our hearts open.

In 1893, several liberal Protestants and Unitarians proposed that there be a World Parliament of Religions as a spiritual component to the Columbian Exposition. The figure who swept through that event and is most remembered to this day was the dynamic disciple of the Hindu saint Ramakrishna, the redoubtable Swami Vivekananda.

In addition, the Japanese Rinzai abbot Soyen Shaku wrote a paper on "The Law of Cause and Effect, as Taught by Buddha," which was read in an English translation by Dr J.H. Barrows, chair of the Parliament. This was the first time on record that an authentic Zen master made a presentation on Western soil. One of those attending was a German émigré to America, Dr. Paul Carus. Carus was fascinated and arranged to meet the Japanese teacher. This would prove to be a fateful encounter.

Carus invited the Zen master to help translate and edit Buddhist texts for Carus's Open Court Press. Soyen Shaku declined, but suggested that Carus hire one of his Zen students, a young scholar named Daisetz Teitaro Suzuki. This suggestion would have incalculable consequences for the establishment of Zen in the West. In 1900, in the same year that Sigmund Freud's *Interpretation of Dreams* was published, Open Court brought out Suzuki's first book in English, *Ashvagosha's Discourse on the Awakening of Faith in the Mahayana.*

This was the first of Daisetz Suzuki's many books. Almost single-handedly, Suzuki would provide an English canon of Buddhist, and particularly Zen, literature. His influence would span the entire twentieth century, and it would be decades after his death in 1966 before many of his translations even began to be superseded.

Because of Suzuki, Zen, while born in China and given unique expressions in Korea and Vietnam as well as Japan, would for the first three-quarters of the twentieth century be known in America and the English-speaking world almost exclusively through Suzuki's Japanese Rinzai perspective. Largely because of Suzuki, even the particular terms we Westerners use for Zen, such as the very word *Zen* rather than *Chan* , come to us in their Japanese versions.

As a writer and teacher Suzuki would influence such people as Alan Watts, who started his own career as a popularizer of Suzuki's more academic presentations. The list of influence goes on to include, but is certainly not limited to, such notables in contemporary Western culture as psychological theorists Carl Jung and Eric Fromm, novelist Aldous Huxley, and poets Allen Ginsberg and Gary Snyder. Once again, from the very beginning Buddhism profoundly influenced the culture it encountered.

The introduction of D.T. Suzuki was not Soyen Shaku's only gift to the West. In 1905 he returned to America, this time bringing with him the young monk Nyogen Senzaki. By this time, there were undoubtedly many Zen practitioners and even Zen teachers among the various East Asian immigrant populations. Still, Senzaki must be counted as the first Zen teacher to both reside in the West and publicly teach those of European and African descent.

To do this, Nyogen Senzaki created a "floating zendo," as he called it, hiring halls as he could afford them, speaking on many different Buddhist perspectives and teaching meditation to those who attended. Among Senzaki's many students was the young American Robert Aitken, later to be known as arguably the foremost Western Zen master of his generation.

Senzaki and Soyen Shaku, while themselves Rinzai, also introduced the reformist Japanese Sanbo Kyodan Zen school to the West, through its teachers Hakuun Yasutani and Koun Yamada. This line of Zen, derived from traditional Soto, but incorporating a complete koan curriculum from the Rinzai tradition, would become one of the most important influences in the shaping of modern Western Zen.

Philip Kapleau, Robert Aitken and Taizan Maezumi were all seminal Western teachers authorized through this lineage. Through their many successors the Sanbo Kyodan, also called the Harada/Yasutani Zen lineage, named for its first two teachers, has marked nearly every aspect of Western Zen.

Here it is necessary to speak briefly of the varieties of Zen. Because Zen is based in part on the idea of lineage, of a line of teacher to student tracing back to the Buddha and Mahakasyapa, various schools have emerged over the generations. Foremost among these are Soto, called Ts'ao-tung-tsung in Chinese, which emphasizes the practice of silent awareness; and Rinzai, or Lin-chi-tsung in Chinese, which emphasizes koan study.

These disciplines will be explored in some depth as we go on. The schools of Zen characterized in their Chinese, Korean, and Vietnamese expressions give slightly different emphases, usually also including some focus on mantric disciplines as well as other elements derived from the Pure Land tradition and other styles of Buddhism.

A number of teachers have helped to shape Zen in the West, particularly in North America, starting in the 1960s. In 1962, Joshu Sazaki brought a strict form of Japanese Rinzai to America. In 1967, Shunryu Suzuki came as a parish priest to serve a Japanese Soto Zen congregation in San Francisco. He would go on to become the founder of the San Francisco Zen Center, one of the most important Western Zen establishments.

In the same year, Taizan Maezumi founded the Zen Center of Los Angeles, which would include a close connection to the Japanese Soto, but also introduced the koan curriculum developed within the Harada/Yasutani lineage. The British-born Soto Zen master Jiyu Kennett came to America in 1969.

The Korean Zen master Seung Sahn arrived in the United States in 1972, assuring that Japanese versions would not be the only types of Zen introduced into the West. At this writing, the number of centers affiliated with his Kwan Um School are second only to those founded by Thich Nhat Hanh and are spread across the Americas. Korean forms were also introduced through the work of the renowned Kusan Sunim, who only visited to lead retreats, and Samu Sunim, who settled in Canada.

The Vietnamese master Thich Nhat Hanh not only assured that Western Zen would reveal its Vietnamese manifestation, but would also be marked by a social justice perspective. Presently living in France, he guides centers in the Americas, Europe, and Africa, the largest network of Zen-related centers in the West. Through his fearless commitment to peace activism and particularly through his collaboration with Robert Aitken and others in forming the Buddhist Peace Fellowship, Thich Nhat Hanh has guaranteed that Western Zen will always be concerned with questions of social engagement.

Chinese forms of Zen were taught in the West by the scholar and meditation master Hsuan Hua, starting in 1962. Unlike most of the Japanese teachers, Hsuan Hua's vision did not include any accommodations for Western culture. Nonetheless, a major translation effort has had considerable influence on the development of a Western Buddhism. Later, another Chinese master, Sheng Yen, would expand Chinese practice styles more aggressively into the Western community.

Of course, this is only a partial list, and does not even include all the "highlights." But through these teachers and their Western successors (and in a few cases today, their successors' successors), Zen is flourishing in hundreds of centers throughout Europe, southern Africa, and the Americas. By the end of the twentieth century, nearly every major form of Zen had at least some representation in the West.

While this book cannot do justice to the complex teachings of the Zen schools, it can provide a brief introduction to Zen philosophy and practice. This book is about how we can discover the true Eden, how we can find ourselves and return home.

# The Teachings of the Buddha

Many of us in the West are hearing the words of Gautama Siddhartha, the Buddha, and creating new meanings for our lives. As we engage this understanding we allow ourselves to be transformed. In this transformation we become transforming forces.

Just as the life of Jesus can be seen as our personal story, so is the life of the Buddha our common human heritage. Like all of us, Gautama Siddhartha was born royal. Each of us is a prince or princess, inheriting all the potential of our human condition. Appropriately for the founder of a great religion, there were many portents at his birth. The sages foretold that he would either be the greatest spiritual teacher the world has known or the greatest emperor of all time. His father saw little glory in his son becoming a religious leader and arranged for his heir's future as a warrior and king. As is often the story, we rarely live up to our parents' desires or expectations; neither did Siddhartha.

The person known to the world as the Buddha was a real human being. He breathed and worked and loved and suffered. When his time came, he died. He was not a god. He was a human being, no more and no less. It takes no denial of Moses or Jesus to embrace the wisdom proclaimed by the Buddha. In a very real way, his enlightenment, his victory over the three demons of greed, hatred, and delusion, is our victory. His story has been distorted by his admirers to the point that it has become a fairy tale about a shining prince who rejected the shams and shadows of the world and discovered true wisdom and the bliss of nirvana. But the myth of the Buddha is the reality of human life. Despite being mixed with fantasies and moral object lessons, the story remains true.

Gautama Siddhartha was born near the end of the sixth century before the Common Era. His father was a chief in the Shakya, one of many small kingdoms nestled in the foothills of the Himalayas in the area that is now Nepal and northern India. He was raised in a privileged situation and seemed destined for worldly success. But something happened. The stories say that he saw four things. First he encountered a sick person. Then he saw someone very old. Then he encountered a corpse. Shaken by these three horrors of life—sickness, old age, and death— he then saw a wandering ascetic. This person seemed to be at peace, beyond the terrors that the worldly life held. These four sights obsessed Siddhartha.

After struggling to ignore the thoughts rising in his mind, he decided to run away from home and seek that enlightenment he believed the renunciant had found. In a disgraceful act that hagiographers have glossed over, he abandoned his wife and child. (This point is especially relevant to western religious liberals because it raises questions about the status of women and children and the place of lay and family life in the practice of Buddhism.)

In a story similar to that of St. Francis and other saints of the east and west, Gautama Siddhartha traded his fine clothing for the rags of a beggar at the gates of his home town. As today, many spiritual teachers were hawking their wares. There were fools and rogues, saints and sages, all promising salvation. After visiting a number of teachers, Siddhartha found one he decided to study with.

He threw himself into the severe ascetic practices that he was studying. His zeal was noticed by the community and the teacher. After a while, his teacher offered to share his leadership with the young renunciant. However, dissatisfied with titles without personal insight into the nature of suffering and a way to actual liberation, Gautama Siddhartha left to continue his search. He worked under another teacher and again was offered a place of shared honor. But Siddhartha was still dissatisfied and went on his way.

For six years he practiced the harshest privations. His ascetic practices impressed other renunciants; eventually five companions joined him in his austerities. He starved himself. Legend says that he subsisted on a single grain of rice per day. Statues of him representing this time show his skin stretched tightly across the bones of his body. He tottered close to death, but still found no peace.

Finally, Siddhartha decided that this way was not going to work either. He got up and wandered into a village where a woman named Sujata gave him a dish of milk and rice and another of honey. His disgusted companions abandoned him to these luxuries. But with his newfound strength, Siddhartha decided to meditate cross-legged in the shade of the bodhi tree. He considered the lessons of his past teachers. He contemplated the sacred writings. He remembered the rituals of the priests. And he let them all go.

He dropped the questions of good and bad teaching, forms and practices, all the concepts he had been taught or derived from his experiences. He surrendered his beliefs that he needed these things. He sat quietly, becoming aware of his breathing and his racing mind and his raging emotions. And he let each go.

Mara, the Buddhist devil, taunted him, sending beautiful maidens and horrible demons and every sort of distraction. All of the supernatural realm knew this was an important event. Powerful changes were going on within the being of this silent human meditator. All the forces of delusion gathered to prevent him from achieving his goal. But he persevered. He continued sitting and his thoughts and emotions began to calm, sinking into a great quiet.

Six days passed. As he looked out at the rising morning star, he understood. He was simply and fully present.

And from this presence he saw the truth of the inter-connectedness of the web of life. He found it not as a valuable philosophical concept, but as simple living and vital truth. He found the very truth about himself and all things. He opened his mouth and proclaimed: "I and all sentient beings of the great earth have in the same moment attained the way." Siddhartha had become the Buddha, the Enlightened One, Shakyamuni, the Sage of the Shakyas.

In the stories, the Buddha's last temptation was to rest in this hard-won wisdom and pass away from the cares of life. But he chose not to turn his back on the world. He found his former companions and proclaimed to them the newly discovered Four Noble Truths. In this manifestation of compassion he opened a way that has engaged millions of people over the ages.

The First Noble Truth of the Buddha is that human life is characterized by a pervasive unsatisfactoriness. The Sanskrit word is *duhkha*, and its usual translation is suffering. This translation is accurate, but not complete. Duhkha means suffering, pain, unsatisfactoriness, angst, anguish. It speaks to a fundamental characteristic of our human condition. The Buddha proclaims this duhkha is a foundational truth of life that cannot be escaped or ignored.

The Second Noble Truth explains the cause of duhkha in *tanha*. Tanha means literally thirst. It points to the human condition, our clinging consciousness. Within the teaching of tanha is the fact that the self is without ultimate substance. Our selves, you and I, are genuine. We do not exist as a dream. We live real, concrete, tangible lives. The human self is real. But our lives are also relative, rising and passing in time. The core of the teaching of tanha is that our perceived self has no ultimate substance; it is empty. Our suffering in the sense of duhkha comes from clinging to what is passing as if it were permanent. But we rarely see this truth about ourselves—that we and all things are conditioned, created through causal relationships, and transient. Our experienced "I"—filled with hope and fear and most of all, desire—clings to passing things as if each were ultimate reality. And as one thing after the other disintegrates, passes away, or dies, the clinging ego is constantly bruised, hurt, crushed, marked by anxiety.

The Third Noble Truth is good news. By direct realization of the insubstantiality of the ego, each of us may know the cessation of duhkha. This emptiness that is our source and end, and indeed our constant reality, is difficult to understand. But when we see into it, we find not a cold withdrawal, but a way of freedom and value. Within the direct knowing of passingness and intimacy, we discover joy and a peace that passes all understanding.

Another way of seeing the insubstantiality and incomparable preciousness of things lies in the reality of their complete interdependence. In Buddhism this mutually dependent universe is sometimes called the Jeweled Net of Indra. The concept appears as the Seventh Principle of Unitarian Universalism, the call for us to acknowledge and "respect the interdependent web of all existence of which we are a part." Even as all things are ultimately empty or void, there is yet an interconnectedness that proclaims the preciousness of these transient things. A Buddhist classic, the *Avatamsaka Sutra*, declares each thing itself the source of the whole universe. It can be said the universe depends on each person, plant, and speck of dust for its existence. We may ultimately be empty, but our particular existence is nonetheless important, valuable, precious. This is all difficult and yet important to understand. In this understanding lies the way to human peace and happiness. The whole Buddhist vision comes from a correct understanding of emptiness and form, samsara and nirvana. The moral consequences of this immaculate void and interdependent universe are far-reaching. Here we realize that personal insight must have a social consequence.

The Fourth Noble Truth presents the vehicle to enlightenment and its realization of suffering, its cause, and its cessation. It is encapsulated as the Eight-Fold Noble Path, consisting of right view, right thought, right speech, right action, right livelihood, right effort, right mindfulness, and right meditation. The Eight-Fold Path is frequently divided into the three interdependent aspects of enlightenment: morality, meditation, and wisdom. The reality that the Four Noble Truths describe is compelling. Each of the Buddha's truths is a powerful statement, as vital to western ears as eastern.

For forty years the Buddha wandered and taught the interconnectedness of all life. As he was dying, the Buddha warned us not to put another's head above our own, not even his. Everyone has full worth in the universe. Each of us is called to see for ourselves and to act in a sacred manner. A human being, Gautama Siddhartha saw clearly into the essential nature of humanity and the universe. He shared his insight by charting a path as valid today as it was 2,600 years ago.

*Buddha Twirls a Flower*

Why are we born? Why do we die? What, if anything, is the purpose of our existence? How do we find meaning in life that is so heavily shadowed by death? It is here in these rich and challenging questions that the faith and practice of Buddhism takes shape and where we find help on our way.

A famous collection of Zen koans—objects of meditation and spiritual exploration in Zen training—called the *Wu-men kuan* includes a story of a large gathering that came to hear a talk by the Buddha. Instead of speaking about enlightenment he simply held up a flower, twirling it slowly in his fingers. Of the whole assembly only one person understood—the Venerable Mahakashyapa. He smiled. Seeing the smile, the Buddha declared, "I have the all-pervading True Dharma, incomparable Nirvana, exquisite teaching of formless form. It does not rely on letters and is transmitted outside scriptures. I now hand it to Mahakashyapa."

In the Zen tradition, this is the foundation of the lineage that connects all teachers with the Buddha.

This story is unlikely to be rooted in historical fact. But that is beside the point. This story illustrates the basics of Zen Buddhism. Truth is transmitted mind to mind, outside of scriptures, outside of written texts. Yet Zen Buddhism is not otherworldly. It is very much concerned with life here and now.

The insights of the Buddha are closely associated with the practice of yoga. In ancient India, the *yogins* claimed to find salvation from the evils of worldly life through the practice of meditation and other structured spiritual exercises. In this period yogins were extremely ascetic. One of the first great Buddhist nuns, Bhadda Kundalakesa, before entering the Buddhist monastic community, was a Jain renunciant. The Jain faith was in many ways similar to Buddhism, but advocated a much more severe asceticism. In that tradition she had her hair torn out as her initiation into the monastic life.

The Buddha sought to reform such practices to eliminate the excessive elements. But his was still a renunciant community devoted to spiritual practice and meditation. The laity were pitied and frequently despised by those who had renounced home and family to seek personal salvation. The monks, and later the nuns, wandered about practicing their meditations and begging for their living. The members of the renunciant community were not seeking salvation in heaven or some other place, but here on earth in their human bodies. In the last analysis the Buddha taught that every person, lay or monastic, man or woman, could achieve liberation, enlightenment.

For many generations, however, the commonality between renunciant and householder was not generally recognized. In fact, it is only in this century and mostly in the West, that a non-monastic Buddhism has become the vital focus of Buddhist communities. For centuries it was strictly understood that the sangha, the religious community, was a prescribed number of monks or nuns and never included lay folk. In spite of this elitist insularity, the tradition remained lively because of Buddhism's teaching that one can achieve enlightenment only within a human body. The question remains: How should we live within the world? We must all wrestle with this question whether we are monastic or not. I have found a hint to the answer. The Buddha offered laypeople Five Precepts as a basis for life in the world: not killing, not stealing, not lying, not misusing sex, and not becoming intoxicated. Over the years, however, these precepts have come to be seen as more than a code of morality. They may be a description of the enlightened mind itself. I will return to this when we explore the use of koans.

Indian Buddhism gradually separated into schools, two of which survive. One calls itself the Way of the Elders, the *Theravada*. Theravadan Buddhism is the Buddhism of Sri Lanka and southeast Asia, except for Vietnam. Many people consider this school the closest to the original Buddhism taught by Gautama Siddhartha. Although academics consider this unlikely, the Way of the Elders represents a profound expression of the Buddha way. *Vipassana*, or Insight Meditation, in addition to being a Zen-like meditation discipline, is also the name for an emerging, western, lay-led movement derived from the Theravadan tradition. In fact, I believe the Western Vipassana community offers the principal alternative to Zen for Western religious liberals.

Here is another example of the spiritual dialogue taking place in the West. In the East these two traditions, Zen and Vipassana, never encounter each other. The cultural gulf between southern and eastern Asia is vast. But in the West, practitioners of these two different schools directly influence each other. Each is a practice of fundamental awareness, but each has evolved unique subtleties and nuances over the centuries. Coming together in the West, each is enriching the other.

The other principal school of Buddhism calls itself the Great Way, the *Mahayana*. The Mahayana emphasizes the Bodhisattva ideal of compassion for all beings and has led to a wide variety of subschools. These schools include such disparate approaches as the faith-oriented Pure Land Buddhism and the individualistic responsibility of *Ch'an* or Zen, as well as the classic syncretism of the *T'ien-t'ai*. Many consider one major variant of the Mahayana, the *Vajrayana*, a third stream of Buddhism. The Vajrayana—the Diamond Way—is the Buddhism of Nepal, Tibet, and Mongolia (with some influence in China and Japan). The various schools of the Mahayana, including Zen, have long existed in China, Korea, Japan, and Vietnam. Now many of these schools of Buddhism are coming to the West. In the Americas and in Europe, Zen is the longest established and probably still the most influential, of the many differing approaches to Buddhism.

Zen is a Japanese word, a cognate of the Korean *Son* and the Vietnamese *Thien*. Each is a transliteration of the Chinese word Ch'an. Ch'an is the Chinese pronunciation of the Sanskrit term *Dhyana*, which simply means meditation. Zen in all its ethnic and cultural varieties is the great meditation school of Mahayana Buddhism. It is primarily within the Mahayana that the possibility of a non-monastically focused Buddhism has gradually presented itself, particularly flowering in the West. It is egalitarian, moderately eclectic, and lay oriented. This is particularly true of the Japanese-derived schools, which have evolved a quasi-monastic, priestly tradition as well as several fully lay-led expressions. There is an important place for monastic Buddhism in the West. Monasticism offers great riches and possibilities for focusing one's practice, which is much more difficult in any other setting. But within this move west, the focus seems to have shifted, and the main area of Buddhism's growth for the near future will likely be in lay and quasi-monastic groups.

Much of my training has taken place in the semi-monastic, priestly Japanese tradition. But today my principal Zen teacher, John Tarrant Roshi, is a lay practitioner rather than a monk or a priest. He represents one of the more dynamic Western Zen schools, the Diamond Sangha branch of the *Harada/Yasutani* lineage. In "The Fortunate and Ongoing Disaster of Lay Life," Tarrant writes of the Mahayana in general, but more especially of contemporary non-monastic Buddhism:

> Now this is quite a different path. The image of enlightenment has changed. The original idea of nirvana was of cessation, extinction, a snuffing out, as of a lamp. Perhaps we should call it endarkenment. It implies a stoic view of things. Life was seen as so contaminated that the end of it was the best thing of all. The Mahayana, and the Zen image is more optimistic: to light a lamp and pass it on. Beings are worth saving, even stones are beings, and consciousness is a great project.

To understand Zen fully we must begin by looking at the movement of Buddhism from India to China. In China the new missionary religion encountered an ancient civilization and the established religious traditions of Confucianism and Taoism. Both of these religions, especially Taoism, transformed and were transformed by Buddhism. This mutual transformation suggests possibilities in the encounters between Zen and Western religions today. Some scholars maintain that Zen is specifically the product of the marriage between Buddhism and Chinese Taoism.

32

It is important to examine the first great encounter between Buddhism and Taoism. Taoism is an unruly nature religion, one that reveres perceived feminine archetypes. Chinese culture despised the "feminine" elements of life and nature—anything weak, dark, watery, passive. The Taoists exalted these elements as the sublime height of spiritual understanding. Taoists played counterpoint to the politically dominant Confucianists in Chinese culture. The cultural elites of the day would frequently be Taoists when they did not possess political power, then Confucianists when in power, and Taoists when they were once more out of power.

Taoism also incorporated folk religion and superstition. While some Taoists produced such spiritual classics as the *Tao Te Ching* and the *Chuang Tzu*, other Taoists spent their energies seeking a physical elixir of immortality, "channeling" various divinities, and buying and selling dubious Masonic-like initiations.

The highly metaphysical Indian Buddhism encountered this earthy and fecund Chinese faith. Astonishingly, each recognized something in the other. The process of dialogue and of synthesis took years. Out of those years of conversation and confrontation came a story. The story is that Indian Buddhism was introduced into China in the sixth century of the Common Era by Bodhidharma, a figure whom scholars consider semi-mythical. According to the traditional Zen lineage, Bodhidharma was the twenty-eighth successor to the Buddha through Mahakashyapa, whom I mentioned at the beginning of this chapter.

Bodhidharma arrived in China after a long and dangerous journey from India. He had an interview with the Emperor Wu, who boasted of the numbers of monasteries and temples he had endowed. The Emperor asked Bodhidharma how much merit he had accumulated. Bodhidharma's reply was terse, "No merit." The emperor was piling his treasure up in heaven, but Bodhidharma wasn't having any of that. Instead he was offering the emperor the saving truth of this very moment.

Enraged, the Emperor demanded, "Who are you?", to which the founder of Chinese Zen replied, "Don't know." Bodhidharma managed to leave with his head on his shoulders and crossed the Yangtze River by sailing across on a reed. Eventually he settled at the Shao-lin monastery where he sat meditating, facing a wall, for nine years.

From the story of that conversation and Bodhidharma's years of wall-gazing comes the tradition called Zen. I will try to explain some of what was meant in Bodhidharma's words to the emperor and what may be found in staring at blank walls. We may find that this story moves into our hearts and becomes part of our own stories.

## Getting Enlightened and Saving All Beings

I was raised a Baptist of the most conservative stripe. In late adolescence I discovered the liberating perspective of Ramakrishna and Vedanta. Not long ago I came across a photograph of myself at eighteen or nineteen, holding a copy of the *Gospel of Sri Ramakrishna* and trying to look spiritual. Today it looks like I may have been suffering from indigestion. When I think of that young man seeking insight, I reflect on the nature of enlightenment and the practices of Zen. On the one hand, frequently too much is made of "enlightenment." Often there is the expectation that this experience provides a permanent transition from unsatisfactoriness to a grand exalted and unchanging state. We fashion a vague dream of broken hearts or unfulfilled desire into something we call enlightenment. And so it becomes an astonishing field of projection. Indeed, this is the problem of literalization, because these concepts are ultimately deceiving. In *Everyday Zen,* the American Zen master Charlotte Joko Beck observes:

Someone said to me, "You know, you never talk about enlightenment. Could you say something about it?" The problem with talking about "enlightenment" is that our talk tends to create a picture of what it is—yet enlightenment is not a picture, but the shattering of all our pictures. And a shattered life isn't what we are hoping for!

In speaking of Zen enlightenment, we must be very careful. Words can set us on the way of liberation or they can become a net of concepts tangling and trapping us. However, we still need to explore the term, "enlightenment," for it is central to the quest, to the decision to take up Zen practice. I offer a description grounded in deeply personal experience from Hakuun Yasutani Roshi:

Enlightenment means seeing through to your own essential nature, and this at the same time means seeing through to the essential nature of the cosmos and of all things. For seeing through to essential nature is the wisdom of enlightenment. One may call essential nature truth if one wants to. In Buddhism, from ancient times it has been called suchness or Buddha-nature or other one Mind. In Zen it has also been called nothingness, the one hand, or one's original face. The designations may be different, but the content is completely the same.

At the same time it can never be reiterated too much: Practice is absolutely necessary. Unfortunately some Western writers, particularly those who have not themselves encountered living Zen, think there is no necessary association between Zen and meditation.

Aside from the etymological difficulty caused by this assertion, the result of such thinking is to reduce Zen to a philosophy of spontaneity, which strikes Zen practitioners as very egocentric. Unfortunately, many would-be students of Zen continue to be misled by a false spontaneity grounded in appetite rather than insight born in disciplined spiritual practice. This is not to say people cannot come to deep insight without engaging formal meditation practice. Occasionally, someone comes to the realization of emptiness and interdependence spontaneously. Even then, however, it is necessary to take up practice afterwards to integrate the experience. Otherwise, there is a great danger that one's insight will simply become a dream or a dim, fondly held memory.

A regular practice is essential to maintain and deepen our realization. The universal guidance of the Zen schools is that meditation and enlightenment are the same thing.

Zen gives us a way of direct encounter with the fundamental questions of human existence. The current popularity of Zen in the West appears to show it has broad human appeal. However, many people begin the practices of Zen, but relatively few persevere. People take up Zen training for many reasons. Some motivations simply aren't strong enough to sustain one over the long haul. It is very difficult to maintain a regular Zen practice. Many people sit once, a few times, or for a couple of years, and eventually give the practice up.

I once heard the Korean Zen master Seung Sahn. During the question-and-answer period someone asked him why people seem rarely to stick with Zen practice for long. He responded that he knew why, grinning mischievously and waiting for a straight line. The questioner repeated, "Why?" And he replied, "Zen . . . Zen is boring!"

Those who take up Zen because they believe the Buddha will endow them with occult powers rarely stick with it. The ordinariness of the practice soon drives them away. Those who take up Zen practice because they want to lower their blood pressure soon discover that the goal is more easily accomplished by sitting down and watching television for a half an hour. They too stop coming to the Zen hall.

Such motivations provide no roots and the practice withers and dies. But many motivations carry the practitioner through a lifetime. In the West there are now many who have practiced Zen for ten, twenty, or thirty years. Some Westerners have lived virtually a full lifetime embracing Zen practice. These people share a characteristic. Their motivations are flexible, changing over the years. If people began by looking for wonders or relaxation, they stayed because they soon discovered that Zen helped them face the deeper issues of life-and-death.

Regardless of the motives that bring people to Zen practice, whether traditional or not—the practice will change them. The change is qualitative. Zen practice is constantly deepening. While there are relatively few Zen practitioners in the West, those who take up this way leaven our many religious communities, enriching all.

## Sitting Zen

The first and most important of the Zen disciplines to be discussed here is *shikantaza* or "just sitting," a practice attributed directly to Bodhidharma. Zenists traditionally claim that it is the practice of Gautama Siddhartha himself. There are no stages to this practice of just sitting or Silent Illumination, but a handful of "techniques" may be used by practitioners at different times in their lives.

Let's begin with a description of the traditional meditation posture. Any number of postures are possible. Although it is even possible to "sit" while lying in a bed, this is discouraged as there is a tendency to float off to sleep when lying down. Those who can maintain the formal postures are doing themselves a disservice by not doing so. The upper torso is to be kept erect if possible. However, those who are bedridden or otherwise unable to conform to the recommended physical postures can do the practice.

The important thing is to engage in the practice as best one can. The Buddha himself seems to have suffered from back problems, probably resulting from a slipped disk. Whatever one's physical condition or physical limits, one can do what is necessary to benefit fully from Zen. All that is necessary is a wholehearted commitment. Ideally, the erect torso is supported by sitting cross-legged with one leg resting on the other, in either the full lotus or half-lotus positions, with the buttocks resting on a *zafu*, a hard pillow traditionally stuffed with kapok fibers from the ceiba tree. It is usually five or six inches high and about sixteen inches wide. Sitting on this pillow allows a downward triangulation of the buttocks and knees that tilts the pelvis slightly forward and supports the torso in a comfortable upright posture.

Few Western adults can attain the full lotus position. Even the half-lotus can be difficult. It is good to try; the discomfort itself can assist in the practice. But it is also possible to sit "Burmese" style with both lower legs crossed on the ground, one leg lying in front of the other, rather than resting on the other. Another way to "sit" is *seiza*, kneeling with the weight supported by resting on a sidewise zafu or a specially designed seiza bench. Backless chairs for computer users that keep the torso erect by tilting the small of the back forward are an increasingly popular western adaptation to the need for correct posture.

Regardless of how one positions the lower part of the body, instructions for the upper torso remain the same. The small of the back is pushed forward slightly and the belly hangs loosely. The head is kept erect and the chin is tucked in slightly. The shoulders are pushed lightly back and the hands are held together in the lap, pressing the torso lightly in the area between the navel and the groin.

When we sit *zazen*, seated Zen meditation, the eyes are kept open. This is most important. In Zen one is not escaping reality, but encountering it in the most intimate way. We are going nowhere else, not to heaven, nor angelic realms, nor to any special place other than here. We are simply allowing ourselves the opportunity to experience the moment genuinely. The gaze should fall to the ground a few feet away, not dwelling on any particular point, but not glazing into indistinction.

When the posture is learned, where to "put the mind" then becomes the most important focus of the practice. The easiest technique and the one most commonly taught is to count the inhalation and exhalation of the breath: "one" on the inhalation, "two" on the exhalation, and so on until "ten." At that point simply begin over again with "one." This may sound easy, but it can be very hard to maintain over a period of time. The mind dances ahead. We lose count. We start thinking about other things: what we should have done that day, what we will do later that day, etc. We encounter what is called a monkey mind, dancing and flying, and doing everything and anything but sitting still and being present.

When we inevitably discover we have lost count, we return to "one." The trouble is that when we discover our attention has wandered, we can easily get doubly trapped by feelings of discouragement, remorse, or anger. It may seem easier to indulge the wandering. It can be very hard simply to return to "one." But to continue the process is to open the door to intimacy and depth.

The scholar and Zen master Ruben Habito speaks of his personal difficulties as an intellectual engaged in Zen training. In *Total Liberation* he writes, "Here I would like to be practical and down-to-earth despite my temperament and background, which tend to leave me hopelessly up in the air at times. What I really want to answer is that, for me, *Zen is simply emptying.*" This is the purpose of all the forms of Zen, to help us in the art of emptying.

Just counting the breath can be a complete spiritual practice. It is a practice to which I constantly return. But after engaging this practice for some time, a month or two, or perhaps a year, people should try other techniques. One may stop counting and instead simply focus attention on the flow of the breath, in and out of the body. Explore this technique at some depth. Months or even years are not too much time to devote to such a discipline. It can reveal much about ourselves and the universe that we occupy. Again, this may be a complete practice for some people.

After doing this successfully over some period of time, without the mind wandering constantly, then attempt simply sitting. Again, while each of these practices may be complete for a lifetime, only this pure sitting is properly shikantaza. In *Zen Mind, Beginner's Mind,* the Soto Zen master Shunryu Suzuki Roshi describes this shikantaza beautifully:

> In this limitless world, our throat is like a swinging door. The air comes in and goes out like someone passing through a swinging door. If you think, "I breathe," the "I" is extra. There is no you to say "I." What we call "I" is just a swinging door which moves when we inhale and when we exhale. It just moves; that is all. When your mind is pure and calm enough to follow this movement, there is nothing: no "I," no world, no mind nor body; just a swinging door.

Great depth comes out of this practice. It is pure and simple and can be taken up with a minimum of supervision. It is wise to connect with a teacher, however, because there are many difficulties along the way. It is hard to learn the posture from a book, and the mind and body also play tricks. It is helpful to join a sitting group to benefit from associating oneself with others in this practice. At the simplest level, the group expects you to attend, which can be a great help through dry periods. There are subtler benefits from joining with others. Companionship on the way is very powerful. We all need support from those who truly share the difficulties and joys of the practice.

But it is possible to maintain a private practice of shikantaza. However we come to sit shikantaza, even for a few minutes, is truly to open the great way. For those who find sitting too difficult or seek to broaden the possibilities of practice there is another practice in walking meditation. This practice largely derives from one of the Theravandan Vipassana disciplines. It is also influenced by the short periods of walking meditation that are common as breaks between sitting periods in Zen training. The Vietnamese Zen master Thich Nhat Hanh is the most widely respected exponent of this simple adaptation of just sitting—what might be called "just walking." In *A Guide to Walking Meditation*, Nhat Hanh tells us:

Mindfulness and peace are the purpose and practice of walking meditation. They need to be continuous, and so we use breath-awareness, stepping, counting, and the half-smile. These four elements bring power to our spirit. They reside in ourselves and reveal the presence of the conscious and all-knowing mind.

By taking a half hour or so every day to just walk about quietly, attentively, one may taste the great way. A single period of Zen meditation usually lasts between a half an hour and an hour, never more. Most teachers in the Diamond Sangha recommend twenty-five minute periods. If one wants to meditate for more than one period, it is wise to get up and stretch or to take a short concentrated walk.

Whether sitting or walking, it is necessary to find a regular practice. The regularity of the practice is essential to its success. Commit some time, just about every day, to learn genuinely what Zen is all about. Half an hour a day, together with a more concentrated period once a month or so, for periods totaling perhaps three or four hours, can be extremely valuable.

It's best if this schedule can be supplemented by attending formal retreats lasting between three and seven days (called *sesshin*, "to touch the mind," in Japanese and *Yong Maeng Jong Jin*, "intrepid concentration," or colloquially "to leap like a tiger while sitting," in Korean), once or twice a year—this is all that is necessary to be a fully committed Zen practitioner.

Whether just sitting or just walking, this is a profound way. Commitment to these practices can enrich our lives in ways about which we have only the vaguest intimation before beginning. Although it is the simplest practice imaginable, this way of simple attention, bare presence, is the path of wisdom, the journey of heaven, the way home.

## Reconciling Heaven and Earth

Over the last few years I have thought a lot about death, perhaps because of my age and circumstances. I am over fifty and somewhat overweight, with very high cholesterol. And I have begun to get little pains in my chest and my arms go numb now and again. When my wife Jan read an early draft of this book, she made me go to our doctor, where an electrocardiogram revealed a "slight abnormality." For the next two days, I thought about the possibilities of death more concretely than usual. Finally, the doctors determined that the "abnormality" was within the range of "normalcy."

That incident focused my thoughts for a while. But all it takes is a twinge in the chest and I feel a flashing panic. I think: I have to exercise; I have to stop drinking so much coffee; I have to eat less and better; I have to write that book; I have to make my mark. My mind races with a flash of panic. It races and races and eventually comes around and I think about death.

Thinking about death has been a traditional motivation for those who stick with Zen practice. Why am I going to die? Why is it that everything that lives has to die? What is death? What does it mean? These questions can drive a person to the deepest introspection, to confront the Great Matter, life-and-death. Three words joined into a single pressing concern: life-and-death. This is the stuff of Zen practice and Zen insight.

Traditionally, another great engine driving the search for wisdom has been the mystery of pervasive suffering. This is the question that drove Gautama Siddhartha in his search. We know that terrible things are going on in the world. War, pollution, starvation, and ignorance threaten human existence and life on the planet. As people of affluent industrial nations, many of our attempts to help others have been piecemeal at best. We watch television and are horrified by scenes of battle, pestilence, or famine. We are perhaps moved to demonstrate against war, to support the troops, to relieve the starving in Asia or Africa. But it does not end. These horrors have always been with us. Only the names and faces change. And it is so easy to become inured to the face of suffering.

Then, having done some little thing and feeling good for a moment, we turn to watch a more pleasant television show. Images of starvation in Africa or the Far East, or of our local homeless people hovering over steam ducts or hiding in the caverns of public transportation, quickly fade from the mind. Even the flare-up of a war is frequently little more than a televised abstraction, ultimately no different than ten thousand other wars, so easily lost with the switch of the channel.

Then we go to bed and must dream. These dreams whisper of suffering and fragmentation and a wholeness that includes the wounds and shadows. A voice tells us the suffering of the world is our suffering. This is a horrible, terrifying intuition. If it is true, then what? What can I do that matters? How can I genuinely help? Is it politics, economics, religion, or something else that will mean something?

Some time ago one of my dearest friends learned that he had cancer. Dan O'Neal was a Unitarian Universalist minister and a longtime Zen student. He dealt with his situation with all the clarity and compassion for self and others for which one could hope. He and his wife Claudia had strong meditation practices. They were also mindful of the saying of the prophet Mohammed, "Trust God, but remember to tether your camel," and explored the range of possibilities for Dan's treatment.

During one of our regular phone conversations Dan put me on the spot, asking me for advice. I tried hard to beg off. I admitted to being a spiritual failure. I acknowledged all my hypocrisies and shortcomings. Dan agreed with all these admissions. He knew me well. But he wouldn't let me off the hook. I had to speak. And for this insistence that I speak, however inadequately, to what I believe to be the fundamental situation, I shall always be grateful. It made me articulate what I believe, truly and completely.

I answered as clearly as I could. As we face the circumstances of our lives, good and ill, it is important that we don't turn away. What we are is the total of all these experiences, all that happens to us and all that we do. Each of our thoughts and feelings is real. Each voice in our being needs expression; each action we take needs notice. The bottom line is we need to attend. However, as we attend, we needn't let any one of these experiences or thoughts rule our lives. What is important is that we broaden the field of our individual consciousness. We need to broaden ourselves so that each thing may stand and walk and have its existence—but not to the exclusion of all the rest.

At the time I served a congregation in the suburbs of Phoenix, Arizona. We lived at the northern edge of the great Sonora desert. When I reflect on this field of consciousness I think of that desert and the vast Arizona sky. This desert is so vast and grand. Saguaro, cholla, and ocotillo cactus dot the landscape. A few head of cattle wander in the distance. A horse stands in the shade of a ragged upshoot of rock. Inca doves and grackles flit in the air. Hidden but present are javalinas, coyote, jackrabbits, geckos, scorpions. No thing dominates. The field and the vast empty sky are too broad, too vast. This is the very field in which I have found zazen.

My Zen practices are aids in helping me widen my consciousness. The process of emptying is not throwing everything away, shutting this or that out. Rather, this emptying is allowing a place for everything. There isn't a lot more to it. However, there are many consequences to entering that broad field. Whatever my motivations may have been as I began this practice, they have not taken me to a spiritually numbing self-satisfaction or narcissism. Instead of focusing the world in on myself, this widening of my consciousness, this broadening of my self, has opened me up to the rest of the world. And the consequences are incredible. This broad consciousness is the mother of compassion, constantly birthing love into the world.

And so I find Dan's suffering becomes mine and his joy becomes mine. This is true even as my suffering and joy are his. This path is a way of intimacy and compassion. I told Dan this was all the advice I had. He didn't seem to mind. Indeed, I think I confirmed his own experience. It is hard to speak to another person's suffering and say anything. Often words betray us at these times. But I believe his understanding is much the same as mine. We truly are joined in the great dance of life-and-death on that vast field, beneath that awful, beautiful empty sky.

That conversation also helped me clarify the relationship between my own experience and the great teachings of Buddhism. I saw how this great way is the source of insight into both emptiness and the phenomenal world. I saw the identity of samsara and nirvana. This field is where the Buddha's insights originate.

Sometime later, I had to cope with a terrible personal situation—my brother had killed himself after being involved in an obsessive and destructive affair involving sex and drugs. This time I found myself asking Dan for advice. And Dan spoke to me from that field. I was comforted by his presence, his broadness of spirit. And interestingly, his living on a field occupied at least in part by cancer and the possibility of imminent death, invited and comforted me as perhaps nothing else could. His words, flowing out of his simple presence, were a great help to me. Knowing that he was simply and fully present to my anguish was amazing.

The great Zen teacher Wu-men tells us that within our practice we become so intimate with the ancestors that our eyebrows tangle together. I surely felt this truth in my meeting with Dan, his words and fully present compassion to my need, in my hurt. The words fail me. But presence abides. And in that presence something beautiful is born. In that field compassion grows like a lovely and fragrant flower. We need to stop, notice, and smell it. Much is revealed in our not turning away.

And such is the nature of our practice. Over the twenty-five years that I've been sitting it has gradually become the most important single thing I do. I've learned a great deal about myself, not all of it pleasant. I'll share some of my experiences in meditation, in the hopes that they will be useful to those considering the practice or to those who have been practicing for a few years.

Even after all these years my mind wanders with great regularity. Those who claim the mind can be stilled to absolute quietness are deluding themselves or lying. The mind is a monkey, always playing, always ready to leap. Complete stillness of mind comes only with physical death. We sometimes achieve *samadhi* states, trancelike or semi-sleep states out of which great feelings of peace and well-being arise. Samadhi states are particularly common during periods of retreat when we devote many hours in a day to concentrated practice. These are good and frequently helpful to us on the way. But they are not the purpose of Zen meditation.

Woody Allen once suggested that most of life is just showing up. One of my teachers added that most of life is showing up prepared. Zazen, seated meditation, is that preparation. This is one reason I like the term "practice" for Zen discipline. It means we are preparing and that we are doing. Zazen is the discovery of ordinary mind. As we sit regularly we discover the noise slows down. And gradually we gain longer periods of quiet reflection, ever purer awareness. But don't make the mistake of idealizing this awareness as something unattainable. In the last analysis Zen is all about ordinary consciousness. The stuff and substance of our practice is ordinariness.

As we cultivate our sitting practice we begin to notice what is going on. We notice how our breath may be long or short, deep or shallow. We notice bodily sensations such as a tingling leg or an itchy nose. We notice our thoughts rise and fall. We may even begin to notice mental patterns, how sex or food or anger are recurring themes to our rising and falling fantasies. As we sit, we notice. The great discovery I made in my sitting practice was of what I call clinging consciousness. As I came to know myself I saw how much I cling. I saw how much I desire, how much I want things and people to be permanent and real and always to be with me.

I find this clinging consciousness raging throughout my being. Indeed, the great burning desire that rises from deep within the neediest parts of myself is a raging, consuming fire. I want. I desire. I cling. This fire burns through everything, consuming all. Over the years, as I sit, I notice this clinging consciousness. I watch it rise. And miracle of miracles, I watch it fall. The fire may return, indeed it will. But it also burns out. And over the years as my practice continues, I discover my clinging dies for a while, to be reborn in new ways, but also a little less fierce. As I sit I even come to understand the clinging. Gradually I've come to know something of what it comes from. I find myself forgiving it and forgiving myself. In my sitting, knowing and forgiving become part of who I am.

Over the years, slowly, compassion rises as an alternative to clinging. I find this a miracle. Such seems to be the nature of sitting Zen: Gradually we come to know who we are, base and silly, broad and noble. Each by turn, me. Each by turn, the universe revealed. There are many lessons along this way. Another is that the three demons of Buddhism—greed, hatred, and ignorance—have a tangible existence. We each have these demons within us or, more correctly, they exist as part of who we are.

As I've reflected on the nature of these demons, I've noticed how one demon tends to lead. For me it is greed. For others it is a clinging, burning anger or fear. And for others it is a profound confusion. The practices of sitting and noticing are the great clarifiers. I've seen how these demons of human consciousness rise and fall. It is a universal experience. In our practice, we notice. And in our noticing we grow slowly more clear, more open, less clinging.

Over the years I've seen so many different feelings and thoughts within me rise and fall. If you are considering taking up this way, here is some of what you may encounter.

Boredom is a hard one, the rock on which many an individual practice has broken apart. The mind is not exactly like a television show, although it has some of the characteristics of a soap opera. However, it has few of the high-tech special effects that carry one's interest to the end of the show. Rather, our minds consist of fairly short tape loops repeating and repeating and repeating. How do we meet this problem? As I encounter boredom in my practice, I note it. I watch it rise; I watch it fall. But I try not to abandon the moment. It will pass with astonishing rapidity without any help from me. Don't indulge the urge to fly away in fantasy. Stick with the boredom. It has a luminous quality and may reveal much.

Another common experience in Zen practice is sleepiness. I've even fallen asleep during morning meditation during retreats. It is astonishing how easy it can be to sleep while in zazen posture. Nodding off is a great distraction, although common to all who have a regular practice. However, if we continue to attend, we can find ourselves noticing sleepiness rise. And in noticing it, it too falls away.

The distractions are limited only by the scope of human possibility. While engaged in sitting practice, one can be engulfed in the passions of judgment. This is a demon that particularly likes me. It's especially easy to get caught in judgment during a practice like breath counting. This plays out in one of two ways, depending on the personal temperament of the individual. For one person, the judgment is directed outward. "If it weren't for the kids upstairs. If it weren't for the cars on the street. If it weren't for them, I would be able to attend and do my practice." Others turn the judgment inward. "I'm too stupid. I have too much bad karma from too many previous lives. I can't do it." Of course, each is a distraction, carrying us beyond that first distraction.

This isn't to say discrimination is unnecessary. To live within the phenomenal universe is to make decisions. As we go through our daily lives, we constantly need to make decisions and distinctions. There are good choices and bad choices. Everything is not lost in a great mush of oneness when we shop for groceries or change a diaper. At the same time non-discrimination, non-judgment, is critical as we sit. It broadens our field of consciousness. It allows us to widen and deepen. It reveals the other half of the great equation: our unity. And from this insight into unity, great emptiness, we may find a perspective that allows our daily decisions to be more compassionate, more accurate. Each thing in its place. The way of Zen is a way of discovering the harmonies of the cosmos, revealed in the shouts of a two year old wanting attention.

While we are sitting, an infinite number of thoughts may rise. If we follow them, they keep us from simply returning to one, to the point of presence. The correct response to any of the myriad things rising in our minds during Zen practice is to notice. When we simply notice, the demons rise and fall, and the field gradually broadens. I can frequently extend this broadness of consciousness out into daily life. I call it "one minute Zen." I'm driving to the church. I notice my breath intake: one. I notice my breath flow out: two. And then a red sports car cuts in front of me: three.

We keep coming back. This is the practice. We keep sitting. And we learn much. At some point we might find restlessness sweep through the mind and body. A great, perhaps a seemingly overwhelming itch may call out for a scratch. We twitch. We feel unstable. A bead of sweat makes its way down the ridge of a nose.

The annoyances can all but drive us to distraction. Again, attention is the great solvent. Attending, paying attention, we discover how wide the mind is, how great is the field of consciousness. And so cancer rises and falls. And so high cholesterol rises and falls. And blood pressure. And the boss. And the job. And the children. And the spouse or partner. All things rise and fall. The difficulty is that we need to be open to each thought, to each feeling. To practice Zen, or any awareness meditation, we must attend to the thoughts that rise and fall. We need to attend to the emotions that rise and fall. Each is legitimate. But none needs to control who we are. Everything rises and falls. In the practice of Zen, we notice it all. And the days and months and years go on. We may discover great and fascinating experiences. Or we may find much of our practice is dryness. We need to notice it all as it rises and falls. And when our attention gets caught up or swept away by a thought or emotion, we simply notice, forgive, and return to the moment: one.

When one has engaged in a serious practice of attention such as zazen for some time, hallucinatory experiences are not uncommon. We may hear voices. We may even see visions. Traditionally in Zen these are called *makyo*, and generally are considered "diabolic" distractions. When one reports a vision to a teacher, the classic response is, "Don't worry, it will pass." Not bad advice. But there is another point: These experiences may be reminders that we are on the way. The point is don't cling. Just attend.

The dryness that eventually comes can be harder. It is the long dark night of the soul. It may come as a groping through a twilight toward light or darkness, we don't know which. We may have been practicing for years. We've experienced the rising and the falling of thoughts and emotions. We keep faithfully to the practice. But we don't seem to get it. We don't find the great breakthrough. We don't achieve enlightenment. Those transformative experiences we read about shrink back into the distance. Instead, we learn about dryness.

Indeed, for many this is the shape of practice year after year. The great dark night is spoken of in all the world's faiths. If one walks a genuine spiritual path one will eventually arrive at the desert. For me this walk into the desert has been a time of greatest discovery, but also greatest despair and fear. It is the same desert as that broad field, but at this time it is easier to notice the circling vultures than the awesome beauty.

As I try to attend, fall into distraction, into the wandering of mind and body, and then return to attention, I feel every emotion of the great desert. I know the parched throat, the burning desire for a drink of cool water. I understand with my complete being the searing of heat, the blinding glare of the sun, the longing aching of body. I've known the desert and I've walked through it. This desert awaits all who undertake the great way.

At these times we especially need our guides and our friends. We must walk the path ourselves, but we have companions. In a discipline such as Zen we may find we are alone together with many others on the way. Here we really learn the value of teacher and community. But even with teacher and friends, still, we eventually find ourselves in the desert.

But it is here in the desert that the great way of Zen is fully revealed. Here we can find what emptiness, *sunyata*, really is. Here we find what each thing really is in its fullness, its absolute naked reality. Here we find the absolute identity of form and emptiness. While standing alone in the desert we find the universal and the particular and learn how they truly are identical.

Many years ago as a young Zen monk, I was eating a meal during a retreat. I was spooning up a thin vegetable soup, gulping each bite. I had come to nothing but broth and still felt the nag of hunger. And I lifted the spoon out of the broth and on top of it was a great cabbage leaf. I almost wept. It was so beautiful. I put it in my mouth. It was delicious. And a great sensation of gratitude for that leaf, for the Zen community, for the whole planet, welled over me.

In a moment I realized how that cabbage leaf, the spoon, the bowl, the stars in heaven, and I were joined and were vacant. Each thing was itself and all were empty. At the same moment, I knew the cabbage leaf as itself and nothing else. And I wept freely, without shame.

Later when I related this experience to the teacher, she responded, "Good, good. Now you have begun your training." Years have passed and I am grateful to say my training is still beginning. Coming to this place of beginning is the very substance of our practice. And this personal discovery of how form and emptiness truly are identical is the beginning of wisdom. It is the way of the sages and the ancients, the realization that may save the many beings.

## Just What Is Nothing?

The spiritual insight that reconciles all things with the great void lies at the heart of my spiritual practice. Here is the identity of samsara and nirvana. Of course, these words fail. This is too grand a statement. I hear my teachers laughing in rebuke and I flush. We can't cling to the words. But the words point to something. Here I think particularly of emptiness, sunyata, and its absolute identity with all things. It is important to unravel a bit the meaning of this Buddhist term sunyata, emptiness, the great void.

Stories often convey the sense of things better than lists or logical formulations. A story sometimes best expresses the truths within one's belly. It was a Monday morning, when we lived in Wisconsin, where I served a congregation in the Milwaukee suburbs. Jan and I were dressing for work. I was tying my tie and complaining that I had to come up with something good for my first contribution to *First Days Record*, a Unitarian Universalist journal. I didn't want to look the complete fool in my first essay. Save that sort of thing for later, I thought. Feeling terribly frustrated, I declared, "What in the world can I write about?"

"Well," Jan replied while putting in an earring, "What about our trip to the Horicon marsh yesterday afternoon?"

"But nothing happened! We didn't see a single goose. Nothing."

"Yes, nothing," she said. "But you go on about 'nothing' all the time. Surely this was a nothing you can do something with. You could call it 'Thoughts on a Wild Goose Chase' or 'Thinking of Nothing.'"

As I pulled on my jacket, I replied "Humph!" But at that moment a secret joy crept into my mind, a secret joy that is the very reconciliation of mind and matter, of form and emptiness, of the world and God. This joy is the release from fear of death, fear of cancer, fear of high cholesterol, fear of every kind. This joy is our true heritage and our authentic home. Nothing and wild goose chases! Indeed, these may well be the most profitable of the things we contemplate in our shared quest for meaning and purpose in life. I believe this "nothing" reveals a genuine joy to be found in the face of all that is.

First, "nothing." Sunyata, emptiness, no-thing. Nothing, the lack of any something. The great mystery of Buddhism: the assertion that all things are empty. And, of course, we also know there is one thing more. Emptiness is said to be the exact corollary to form, to the realm of things.

For many people this is an intriguing thought, particularly in the light of contemporary physics. But we are not talking about philosophy. We are discussing finding meaning in our lives, discerning the true nature of the cosmos and the human heart. This nothing is the most important thing we may ever come to know. This nothing can be approached in any number of ways. After we first notice the possibility, it seems we frequently circle around this nothing like animals around a fire. It catches the eye; it raises the imagination. Indeed, the very mysteriousness of it fires all sorts of ideas. In the great irony of existence, we end up looking for some nothing that is something.

Of course, when we think about it, any "thing" is not nothing. Nothing means simply nothing, no-thing. As we consider what this word might point to, we find it may be the empty ground of our being. Certainly it is that from which we come in birth and that to which we shall return at death. And, my teachers assure me, this nothing is as well the substance of everything we do and are between birth and death.

The proof of this pudding must be found in the tasting. So, here I think about Jan and me driving through the countryside of southeast Wisconsin, on our way to a great marsh, allegedly the resting place of a hundred thousand migrating geese. Since we found no geese, our quest for the multitude of wild geese became our wild goose chase. A chase where we found nothing. Not a goose in the marsh. As I reflect on it, I see our nothing was filled with somethings, all sorts of somethings. There was the drive itself, filled with our companionship, our conversations. There were the fading colors of late autumn and small lakes so incredibly blue they should defy all but the greatest artists. The upper Midwest is astonishingly beautiful.

The sky was filled with another blue simply beyond my ability to word-paint. And clouds—the changing dance of each making my heart dance with them. We drove by people buying pumpkins from outdoor vendors and farms with cows standing near fences, staring at us while chewing their cuds. Our nothing was filled with some-things, many precious and wonderful somethings. Within this encounter is the nothing of Buddhism. Not abstract truths that we may call nothing, but an intimate experience of reality, with little filtering through the monkey mind.

Here, right here, I find a nothing that allows the everythings. By just letting be, I find a simple presence that allows passingness, an ultimate nothingness to things. In allowing things to be passing, beautiful, and precious, I encounter perspective. This perspective may be helpful to many of us. For me this was another rediscovery of a nothing revealed in letting go of the bustle and stress of work, letting go of planning and preparing—and just plain simply being with. I was just being with Jan. I was just being with the cows and the pumpkin patches and the dry corn stalks filling the fields as we drove by. Nothing big, no big deal. Yet, it was a nothing allowing everything, a nothing that allowed joy.

There was something in this nothing for me. The preciousness of the moment, realized. The value of companionship, rediscovered and rediscovered again. This showed a presence that needs no reward, no accomplishment, no finish, shining forth just as it is. This was quite a nothing, a precious and wonderful nothing. I think about how I almost missed it and I gasp at my good fortune. All the Zen sitting I've done allowed me to notice. This is what Zen is all about, noticing what is revealed in this very moment. We can be so caught up in the details of our lives, the things that need doing right now, that we end up missing such a lot. Perhaps we miss too much. Children grow and are gone. A loved one dies. A friend moves across the country. Things and people pass so quickly. It is easy to miss life's joys, both small and great.

We need to stop once in a while and notice the nothing. ("Where did you go?" "Out." "What did you do?" "Nothing." Our teachers rise whenever we are ready.) When we notice the nothings, we may even discover the wisdom of a wild goose chase. It doesn't require a drive in the countryside. We can find our nothings in a walk in our neighborhood, even in very mean streets. The great way has profound consequences for those who care about social justice. It reveals much that can guide us in our choice of actions. But first we need to learn that no place should be despised, no moment denied. In nothing everything becomes equal. High and low only exist in the world of something. We need to sit and to discover nothing.

Out of this common nothing I discover joy may be found anywhere. It may be revealed while sipping a cup of coffee in the kitchen. We might even find it in a reflective pause at work. I've even noticed it in church committee meetings. We may find it in a still moment attending tragedy or great loss. This nothing is all around us. It is an amazing cornucopia. Our personal discovery of this nothing is the point of spiritual practice.

*An Impossible Question*

A direct personal realization of emptiness and interdependence is absolutely necessary in Zen. It is necessary for any of us to have this, whatever name we call ourselves, if we really want to understand how things are. It is the way of release from suffering. It is the hint of how we may act together. It reveals the holiness of all things. And it is the point of zazen, of all the difficulty and pain of sitting. Shikantaza, just sitting, is a truly powerful spiritual discipline. And it is a complete practice. Over the centuries people have grown deep and wise engaging the ways of clarity and attention. For some, however, including me, the completely unique Zen practice of koan study was necessary to truly encounter the identity of form and emptiness. In my own practice it was not until I entered the koan way that I fully experienced just what those words—emptiness and interdependence—really mean. This part of the book looks at form and emptiness, primarily by examining the koan way in Zen. The direct personal realization of form and emptiness is called *kensho*, a Japanese term meaning "to see into one's true nature." It is synonymous with another famous term, *satori*. Satori derives from the Sanskrit verb *satoru*, "to know." This is not the knowledge of accumulated facts, but gnosis, insight or wisdom. This knowledge or insight or clear seeing is our fundamental human heritage. It is accessible to anyone, whatever their religion or spiritual practice. This clear seeing is most closely associated with the practice of koan study and sustained by shikantaza, just sitting.

I want to introduce the basic concepts behind koan work. Practitioners engage in six types of koan over the years. They are the *hosshin, kikan, gonsen, nanto, goi*, and the Precepts. The first, hosshin, addresses absolute reality, sunyata, emptiness. The second, kikan, addresses how differentiation expresses itself within emptiness. The next two, gonsen and nanto, deal in differing ways with the complexities of interrelatedness between form and emptiness. This koan has been at the heart of my spiritual path. And now as a Zen teacher I continue to find koans an ever deeper way into the mystery.

I will mainly discuss the first two categories. The hosshin and kikan koans particularly encapsulate the fundamental issues of Zen study. I will simply outline the last four categories, as an introduction to the subject. I undertake this enterprise with trepidation. Even people with a deep knowledge of Buddhism do not necessarily understand koans. Pure Soto Zen teachers who have for the most part abandoned formal koan training, frequently make misinterpretations in their talks, some of which are published. Most of these teachers have not trained with koans and they frequently treat them as metaphors for enlightenment. This approach is not without value, but neither is it using koans as they were intended. Rather, when properly used in the context of formal spiritual discipline, koans confront us directly with the true nature of reality.

John Tarrant Roshi notes, "In koan work we are given a question that is impossible. This question is life. We are given instructions that are vague and inadequate by necessity, since they are intended to turn us inward. They support us not in belief but in discovery."

To answer a koan "correctly" is not to become "enlightened." It is similar to many experiences we all have had in our lives that must properly be called "enlightening experiences." I've found this a valuable term, suggested by another of my guides and friends along the great way, the Zen teacher Tundra Wind. As a spiritual discipline, koans can nudge and push our consciousness. They allow us to find our own experience of something that thousands of other people in many cultures and different times have discovered. The goal of all koan work is the goal of all spiritual practices. Indeed, for many Westerners, here we find nothing less than what Jesus called the Kingdom of God, the Realm of Heaven. It is here that we find our true home.

Historically, most koans come from the public disputes of Zen practitioners during the T'ang dynasty in China, between the seventh and tenth centuries of the Common Era. Literally, *ko* means public and *an* means case; koan means a public record. Probably the simplest definition of koan is "a 'problem' given by a Zen master to a practitioner to lead [her or] him to self-awakening."

However, thirteenth-century Zen master Dogen Zenji gave an eccentric yet illuminating interpretation of the words *ko* and *an*. As Masao Abe and Norman Waddell record this interpretation, "the ko of koan means sameness or ultimate equality that is beyond equality and inequality, and an refers to 'keeping to one's sphere (in the universe).'

"Koan thus indicates the individuality of things and their absolute equality, the sameness of things' differences, the difference of things' sameness." They suggest that a koan points to the ultimate reality of sunyata and simultaneously to the distinct individuality of each thing in its suchness. All this is distilled in the American Zen master Robert Aitken's comment in *The Gateless Barrier* that koans are "stories and verses that present fundamental perspectives on life and no-life, the nature of the self, the relationship of the self to the earth and how these interweave."

In the Sung period, between the tenth and the thirteenth centuries of the Common Era, the more famous koans were gathered into the great collections such as the *Wu-men kuan*, the Gateless Barrier (or *Mumonkan* in Japanese), and the *Pi yen lu*, the Blue Cliff Record (in Japanese the *Hekigan-roku*), and the *Ts'ung-jung-lu*, the Book of Serenity (*Shoyo Roku* in Japanese). The traditional count claims 1,700 koans. In most schools somewhere between five and six hundred koans are explored in depth.

Most koans have multiple questions to be addressed. Each of these takes the form of a particular word or phrase called a *hua-tou*, or in Japanese a *wato*. In "Chao-chou's Dog," which we will explore, the wato is the word *Mu*. Many koans have several wato, each needing to be met by the student, with the results of this meeting confirmed by the teacher. This need for the guidance of a teacher may be the greatest difficulty for those who wish to take up koan Zen. While anyone may practice just sitting with a minimum of supervision, it is impossible to study koans without a qualified teacher. Fortunately, there are an increasing number of such teachers in the West. However, if you are considering studying with a teacher, I strongly suggest that you learn something about the character and reputation of that person. Do not be satisfied simply with finding a name in a magazine advertisement or the yellow pages. Unfortunately, not every Zen teacher is a good one. There are frauds and people of questionable moral character. And there are people with legitimate formal qualifications who simply aren't good teachers. It is not hard to find out about the reputation of teachers. As the Sufi sheikh and Zen teacher Samuel Lewis said when asked how to find a spiritual director: "Keep your heart open, but also keep your eyes open."

Koans are not riddles. Koans are not conundrums. Koans are not paradoxical questions. At the same time, koans are riddles, conundrums, paradoxical questions. To find what koans genuinely are—the real value of koans— we need to shake loose our conceptions and allow ourselves simply to experience the event as it presents itself. Koans may best be said to be "immediate pointings to reality." Aitken Roshi once observed that if you ask an eleven year old what a train is, she is likely to say something like "It's big and runs on tracks." Perhaps less technical, but not much different than what an adult might say. But ask a four year old and she may burst into a "chug, chug, beep, beep" demonstration. The train, here, now. Koans are no different. The question is a statement, now. The answer is a demonstration, now.

This direct and concrete approach to the great questions of life has been seen in Western culture. For instance, James Boswell in *Life of Johnson* recounts:

After we came out of the church, we stood talking for some time together of Bishop Berkeley's ingenious sophistry to prove the non-existence of matter, and that everything in the universe is merely ideal. I observed that though we are satisfied his doctrine is not true, it is impossible to refute it. I shall never forget the alacrity with which Johnson answered, striking his foot with mighty force against a large stone, till he rebounded from it, "I refute it thus!!"

Not too much emphasis should be given to such an example of "direct pointing." While it looks very Zen, this demonstration is only partially true. As the physicist and Anglican theologian John Polkinghorne points out in *One World: The Interaction of Science and Theology*, "Dr. Johnson kicking the stone to refute Bishop Berkeley will not do. That stone is almost all empty space and what is not is a weaving of wave-mechanical patterns." Still, keeping context in mind, Johnson's wonderful kick hints at how within koan study one must directly engage with body and mind the great questions of life-and-death. This illustration shows us that we must directly embody our understanding.

Koans guide us to that place where we have a personal self-awakening, direct knowing, which is kensho. Most people take up koan study with one of the *Dharmakaya* or hosshin koans, the koans of absolute reality. Perhaps the most famous of the Dharmakaya koan is "Mu":

A monk asked Chao-chou, "Has the dog Buddha nature or not?"
Chao-chou said, "Mu."

Mu means no. The only additional information that might help anyone who takes up this koan is to assume the monk is an old Zen hand and knows full well the doctrinally "correct" understanding that all things have Buddha nature, true nature. What the monk seems to ask is, "If even a dog, which is treated as vermin in this culture, can have

Buddha nature, can it be that I, too, genuinely have Buddha nature?"

Chao-chou's Mu fills the universe. There is no space in it for a second thought or even a second breath. Mu opens heaven and earth, and if completely grasped, shows us that kensho is simply discovering who we are since before the creation of the stars and planets and who we shall be long after the stars and planets die.

Mu is the necessary starting point. It refers to the ultimate emptiness called sunyata on which so much of Buddhist understanding is predicated. There is a traditional Zen saying: "When I first undertook the way, I saw that mountains were mountains, and rivers were rivers. As I deepened in my practice, I saw that mountains were not mountains, and rivers were not rivers. Finally, as I came to a fuller realization, I saw that mountains are mountains and rivers are rivers."

This suggests the direction of Zen training. At first we live with a naive discrimination. I am me. You are not me. An ethic comes out of this understanding: As I am the subject and you are the object, what is good for me is right and what you need is subordinate to my needs. I act upon you and ultimately what I need can be taken from you.

The discovery that mountains are not mountains and rivers are not rivers is startling. It is the realization that things are not as we had thought before. It is the first intimation of emptiness, a profound discovery, the awakening to Mu, to the Dharmakaya, to Absolute Nothingness.

In the Harada/Yasutani Zen lineage there are more than twenty traditional Dharmakaya koans that a Zen student will be asked before moving on to a collection called "Miscellaneous Koans" and then the traditional collections, the *Wu-men kuan*, etc. They include such questions as "How high is Mu?", "What color is Mu?", and "What is the source of Mu?", and several questions based on another famous koan: "Hakuin Zenji used to ask his disciples: 'What is the sound of the single hand.'"

These cases guide us to insight into our essential unity within emptiness. However, we cannot stop here; we must also see into the realm of differentiation and we will with the next category of koans. Zen understanding is frequently thought to be seeing into sunyata, the shining emptiness of the cosmos and everything in it. This is true, but if we stop there it represents a one-sided understanding. In the *Heart Sutra* we hear "form is no other than emptiness, emptiness is no other than form."

Still this insight into emptiness is foundational. The Dharmakaya koans allow us to see into the truth that form is no other than emptiness. We may have an intellectual understanding, but is it really clear? Do we really know what this means? When we engage Mu or any of the other Dharmakaya koans, we engage absolute nothingness. We engage it, however, not as philosophers or theologians, but as ordinary people with deepest personal connection to the question. It is the fundamental question of where do we come from and where do we go? It becomes a burning molten rock stuck in our gullets that we can neither swallow nor vomit up. Does a dog have Buddha nature? Mu! Do I have Buddha nature? Mu. Mu!

The remarkable Zen teacher and philosopher Keiji Nishitani tells us in *Religion and Nothingness:* "Nothingness is not a 'thing' that *is* nothingness." We must surrender all our concepts and enter into a direct knowing. The koan is one way to do this. This path is fraught with dangers. In *Zen and Western Thought* Masao Abe, considered to have inherited Daisetz Suzuki's mantle as the great scholarly interpreter of Zen to the West, warns of an "erroneous understanding of and attachment to Emptiness (which comes as) a result of conceptualizing it." It is possible to miss the whole thing in a mass of concepts or visions or emotions.

Any attempt to attach a static quality to Mu is to freeze truth into a lie. Mu is dynamic. Abe Sensei writes, "This existential realization that true Emptiness 'empties' itself indicates that it is not a static state which is objectively observable but a dynamic activity of emptying in which everyone and everything are involved."

We must completely commit ourselves in the question, Mu? We must completely lose ourselves in the statement, Mu! When we see Mu here and Mu there and Mu and Mu and Mu—then, in an event both generated by "self-power" and by "other-power," the whole of heaven and earth shakes and we laugh at our foolishness and cry at the wonder of it all. Here we find Bodhidharma's "don't know." Mu.

Don't know. When we discover Mu we discover who we really are. If we understand this one question, then we will discover the truth of Wu-Men's verse:

Gateless is the Great Tao
There are thousands of ways to it.
If you pass through this barrier,
You may walk freely in the universe.

Robert Aitken writes of how his own teacher "Yamada Roshi used to say that he read [this case] constantly, and each time found something new. This is a hint about Mu as well, for this koan is not a raft you discard when you finally make it your own. I am still working on Mu, a great mystery, though it is no longer alien."

## The Power of Words

The kikan, or koans of differentiation, help us fully under-stand that emptiness is nothing other than form. Abe Sensei points out that "it is necessary and indispensable for true liberation to 'empty' Emptiness as the final step." One classic kikan koan is, "All things return to the One. To what does the One return?" Here we come, not exactly full circle, and discover with those new eyes that mountains are in-deed mountains and rivers are indeed rivers.

In *Zen Koan* Miura and Sasaki say, "With the help of the kikan koans we release ourselves from the bonds that hold us fast, get out of the sticky morass in which we are floundering, and return to the unfettered freedom of the open fields." Another example given in *The Gateless Bar-rier* of the kikan koans is "Tou-shuai's Three Barriers":

The priest Tou-shuai set up three barriers in order to examine his students:

"You make your way through the darkness of abandoned grasses in a single-minded search for your self-nature. Now honored one, where is your nature?

"When you have realized your self-nature, you are free of birth and death. When the light of your eyes falls, how are you free?

"When you are free of birth and death, you know where to go. When your four elements scatter, where do you go?"

We'll return to the kikan koans and this particular case later. First I want to summarize the other types of koans. The third category of koans are the gonsen, literally "the study and investigation of words." The teachings of the ancestors can liberate us or bind us as tightly as any chains. Within a single word or phrase we may find life and death revealed. So within our single response, we may find ourselves caught in the web of delusion or revealed to be standing free within the cosmos. The gonsen koans take us to an ever deeper understanding of the great play of emptiness and form.

The fourth category of koans are called nanto or "difficult to pass through." Included in *Zen Koan* is what Hakuin Zenji, the great reformer of koan Zen in Japan, wrote of the nanto koans,

My advice to you eminent persons who study this profound teaching is this: You resolute [ones] must dauntlessly display your spirit and attain insight into your real nature once. But, the moment your insight into your own nature has become perfectly clear, discard the insight you have attained, and settle these nanto koans. Then you will understand beyond the question of a doubt the words of the *Nirvana Sutra* when it says: "All the Buddhas and World Honored Ones see their Buddha-nature with their own eyes as clearly as they see the mango fruit lying in the palms of their hands."

Next come the goi koans, or the koans of the Five Ranks. The Five Ranks are sometimes said to present the "philosophy of Zen." But remember that it is a mistake simply to read a description of koans and to believe from that reading one has a genuine insight into Zen. One must pass through many koans before one can truly appreciate the depths of the goi koans. Originally developed in the Soto school, these koans are considered the penultimate koans of *Rinzai* Zen. I find this an interesting conundrum for those who say Soto Zen is alien to the koan way.

Adapted from the Chinese classic *I Ching* by the Soto founder Tung-shan Liang-chieh, the Five Ranks are sometimes pictured as circles. It is possible to see how they recapitulate the statement, "Form is emptiness, emptiness is form," showing the permutations of these two truths. They consist of two elements, *cheng* (in Japanese, *sho*) meaning "the straight," and *p'ien* (in Japanese, *hen*) meaning "the bent."

Here they represent the absolute and the relative emptiness and form, the two realities with which we live. The Five Ranks include the bent within the straight, the straight within the bent, the coming from within the straight, the arrival at the middle of the bent, and unity attained.

Finally, one takes up the precepts as koans. Once again, it is necessary to consider the line from the *Heart Sutra*, "Form here is only emptiness, emptiness, is only form. Form is no other than emptiness, emptiness no other than form." The same absolute nirvana of Buddhism is this phenomenal world. This is the foundational insight of Zen. But for it to have value, it must be encountered wholly with one's being.

A one-sided view is functional blindness. Everything must be discovered here and now. The sky is blue, the leaves are green. The literal, the compassionate, and the essential are all encountered now in this place, by us—you and me. We are constantly confronted with the situations of real life. The precepts cannot remain abstractions if they are going to be of use to us in our daily lives. They must be the stuff of our actual encounters, intimate and immediate. But we are no longer compelled to treat morality as rules imposed from above. We can move beyond a morality based in a shallow dualism.

The Five Precepts are not killing, not stealing, not lying, not misusing sex, and not becoming intoxicated. As I suggested, they can be seen as the very expression of Zen enlightenment. Through the negation of negation, we can move beyond dualism and emptiness. Here we find ourselves awakened, as Abe Sensei writes, to "the realization of true Emptiness [which] is the basis for human freedom, creative activity, and ethical life." Here those precepts are revealed as really expressing the fostering of life, respecting things, speaking truthfully, honoring our bodies, and seeing clearly into the life of the world and ourselves.

Within the Zen schools, as in other Mahayana Buddhist communities, we gather these Five Precepts with others to make the sixteen Bodhisattva precepts. The others include the three refuges within Buddha, Dharma, and Sangha; the three so-called pure precepts: cease from evil, do good, and do good for others; and additional precepts added to the traditional five, which differ slightly from school to school.

In the Diamond Sangha the precepts are not discussing the faults of others, not praising yourself while abusing others, not sparing the Dharma assets, not indulging in anger (or hatred), and not defaming the Three Treasures—the Buddha, Dharma, and Sangha.

Again, although they are phrased negatively, these precepts can be understood as positive expressions of the enlightened life. But proper direction is needed. Correct understanding is found first by discovering emptiness; only then can the richness of our condition be discovered as we empty out of emptiness. Koans must be personal, deeply personal, intimately personal. They reflect our most fundamental truths and must be engaged with all the energy we have. It is necessary to return to the question of emptying our emptiness. When we have understood Mu, what then do we understand about death? Here the kikan koans are very important. This is why I will next return to the set of kikan koans called Tou-shuai's Three Barriers.

In the Zen curriculum of the Harada/Yasutani school, we first encounter Tou-shuai's Three Barriers near the end of the "Miscellaneous Koans," where they count as the seventeenth of twenty-two cases. We face them again near the end of the *Wu-men kuan,* as the forty-seventh of forty-eight cases. Taken together they are called in the Harada/Yasutani school the "deathbed koan." In fact, even though there are three questions, they really are one question and are counted as one in the collections. Here is another translation from *Mumonkan* using the Japanese form of Tou-shuai's name, Tosotsu:

> The Priest Tosotsu set up three barriers in order to examine his students:
>
> "We make our way through the darkness of abandoned grasses only in search of self-nature. Now, honored one, where is that nature?
>
> "When you have realized your nature, you are surely free of birth and death. When the light of your eyes falls, how are you free?
>
> "When you are free of birth and death, you know where to go. When your four elements scatter, where do you go?"

Tou-shuai Ts'ung-yueh was a teacher in the *Lin-chi* or Rinzai Zen lineage of China. He entered the religious life as a boy and studied in both of the major schools of Buddhism, the Theravada and the Mahayana. Turning to Zen, he trained with a number of masters before meeting his teacher Pao-feng K'o-wen, under whom he achieved enlightenment. He died in 1091 at the age of forty-eight.

In ordinary terms his life was cut short—he was a vibrant teacher with great potential. But in reality he died at just the right time. Indeed, this is something we too must find, the right time. This right time is one of the great teachings of Zen. Check your pulse; notice your breath.

Let us take up the wato in order. First, "We make our way through the darkness of abandoned grasses only in search of self-nature. Now, honored one, where is that nature?" This wato speaks to the quest for realization. In this way there is great stress put on kensho—sometimes crudely termed "enlightenment," but perhaps better called intimacy.

We are each of us called from the foundation of the universe to realize our own true nature. Part of the irony of this way is that it takes great commitment and great searching—only to take us to the point where we must throw away the clinging. The answer to the first part of the question lies within the search itself. What foundation? What universe? What self-nature? What clinging? With all our hearts and minds we must throw ourselves into the search. No stone must be unturned, no nook or cranny unexplored. If you understand this, then all the questions are answered.

Now a little on the second wato in this case. Jan and I have a friend, Bob Jessup, who died of AIDS. We went to say goodbye not long before he died. After visiting with him for a very short time, his energy gave out and we went out to the front room to talk with his partner, Tundra Wind, a Zen priest who leads a small sangha in California's Sonoma County. Tundra was telling us about some of the things Bob said in those last few days, as his death became more imminent. Bob was very weak, at a point where he ingested only fluids. His body was completely wasted. Tundra was sitting with Bob and talking about the good times they had had. Bob looked up at him and said, "I'm still having a good time." This statement is more than a hint for this whole koan. One hundred percent into the search, a hundred percent into the present.

Now the second wato: "When you have realized your nature, you are surely free of birth and death. When the light of your eyes falls, how are you free?" When you are dead, how are you free? To correctly answer the first part is to be drawn irresistibly into knowing the answer to the second. Death. Have we gone raging into the dying of the light? Has our last breath flown as gently as a dove's wing from our nostrils? Right then, at that moment, how are we free? We must find our death. We must claim our death.

The Sufis say that one must die before one dies. This is the center of the Christian story of the death and resurrection of Jesus. To have eternal life, a person must die in Christ. As Paul tells us, "I have been crucified with Christ; it is no longer I who live, but Christ who lives in me." It has nothing to do with individual ego survival, but speaks of something radically different, more valuable. What is the point? Death and freedom. Freedom and death. Shakespeare speaks eloquently of how we are free within death: "So shalt thou feed on death, that feeds on men. And death once dead, there's no more dying then."

Finally, the third wato: "When you are free of birth and death, you know where to go. When your four elements scatter, where do you go?" Ah, the big question! The nut at the core of all cosmological speculation. This reveals the motivation that drives this koan. When we "cast off this mortal coil," then what? I don't believe in the survival of the individual ego consciousness after death in a literal sense. Others believe in personal survival after death. Who is right? More to the point, who knows? As our friend Bob was dying a number of people came to visit him. When we saw him, Jan said that we "just wanted to say goodbye." He replied that half of western Sonoma County had been by to say goodbye. We had all come carrying our baggage. Encountering a dying person is like encountering a Zen master. It is all out on the table. All our secrets are plain for anyone who cares to notice. Our words and our silences, our discomfort, our ease, all speak volumes.

Tundra told us how people came to Bob, all wanting to "assist him in the transition." Some were into Tibetan

Bardo teachings, others into the profound truths offered by Elisabeth Kubler-Ross or Stephen Levine. Others—who knows what they wanted to offer? Bob would listen to these people, thank them, and ask them not to return. Frequently people were flabbergasted. One person was angry and insisted that Bob "needed to process what was going on." Bob replied, "I don't need to process anything. I am the process."

I am the process. To understand this is to understand the koan and all the koans. In *Margaret Fuller,* Paula Blanchard writes about the Transcendentalist Margaret Fuller as exclaiming to the poet Thomas Carlyle, "I accept the universe." Later, writing about this, he commented, "By Gad, she'd better!" Both are right and both point to the meaning of this koan: intimacy, intimacy.

No credos of any sort. No "I believe." The question and the answer demand direct encounter. The boy holding his treasured copy of the *Gospel of Sri Ramakrishna,* the young man with aching knees sitting through a seven-day retreat who discovers the universe in a cabbage leaf, and the middle-aged man learning that his brother has committed suicide, are one in the direct experience of the moment. We cannot abandon our history. Zen does not call us to do so. But we must attend fully to this moment. This is a call to complete intimacy.

"When your four elements scatter, where do you go?" When you die, where do you go? In "The Problem of Death," Abe Sensei wrote, "Yet the problem of death, no matter how much words are piled up, cannot in the end be touched in its reality. In reference to the question of birth-and-death, as Tao-wu answered to the question of Chien-yuan, 'I won't tell! I won't tell!' must be the only correct answer."

Our prose becomes impoverished in the face of such a question as life-and-death. Here we must discover the truths that can be conveyed only by the poetry of words or actions.

*Returning to the World*

We look up at the morning star, and with the same voice as Gautama Siddhartha we say, "Oh, wonderful! Wonderful! Now I see that all beings of the universe are the *Tathagata!*" We are all the Buddha, the "thus come one." Here, now, we are home.

As we attempt to walk responsibly on this planet, we need perspective. If we hope to make a difference, we need a place from which to act. The specific insights of Buddhism and the perspective to be found in Zen practice are ideal for many Westerners. What is this perspective? What are the Buddhist insights that can make our lives deeper and more productive? This is the purpose of zazen and koans: I walk down to the corner store and get a quart of milk. I sit in the playground and sing a silly song with the children.

In that magnificent map of genuine intimacy, *The Ox and His Herdsman*, the eighth circle is "Complete Oblivion of Ox and Herdsman" and shows an empty circle. The ninth circle is "The Return to the Ground and Origin," and shows a scene of untampered nature. But the tenth and final picture, showing a fat man with a bag entering a village, is titled "Entering the Market with Open Hands." The point is to return. To find our depth is to return to daily life. We wander the world to find that wisdom is always here, it is always right at home. This is the secret of the Zen way. We sit quietly or walk quietly; perhaps we engage koans; we visit with a friend. To sit on a hillside with the rivers and the earth, the grasses and the trees, and enjoy that full round moon shining overhead, is the fullness of Zen, and indeed, the fullness of our humanity.

The point of Zen is just this: emptying. And out of this emptying, returning—returning home. Our personal identities are exactly identical with the great emptiness. We must learn this truth with our bodies and with our minds, complete. To find genuinely open hands we must come to know ourselves. There is a great deal to this returning with open hands. There is an ethic of enlightenment. There are many consequences to our realization that in one aspect of genuine reality, we are all one. I've alluded to some of those consequences in my consideration of the precepts. When we truly attend we may discover some of how it can be done profitably. The way of intimacy is a way of respect and beauty and grace.

All I want to do at the conclusion of this book is to remind you, my friend, of the beauty and grace of this moment. This is home. This very place is where we find wisdom. This moment reveals what needs to be done and what can be left alone. Whatever traditions we claim, whatever religion we embrace, this moment shows its truth.

This right-here-and-now moment is the great play of existence, of life and death, of all that was and is and shall be. This very moment is both the doorway to heaven and heaven itself. Our teachers and friends who have walked the way before stand at the door, beckoning to us. They give us a broad wink; a crooked finger wiggles at us, beckoning us, welcoming us.

All we need do is step through.

p. 27 **I have the all-pervading True Dharma:** Zenkei Shibayama, *Zen Comments on the Mumonkan* (San Francisco: Harper & Row, 1984), p. 58.

p. 32 **Now this is quite a different path:** John Tarrant Roshi, "The Fortunate and Ongoing Disaster of Lay Life," in *Mountain Record,* Volume XII, No. 2, Winter 1993, p. 22.

p. 34 **Enraged, the Emperor demanded, 'Who are you?':** Thomas and J. C. Cleary, Translators, *The Blue Cliff Record,* Volume One (Boulder: Shambhala, 1977), p. 1.

p. 36 **Someone said to me, "You know, you never talk about enlightenment":** Charlotte Joko Beck, *Everyday Zen* (San Francisco: Harper Collins, 1989), p. 173.

p. 36 **Enlightenment means seeing through:** Heinrich Dumoulin, *Zen Enlightenment: Origins and Meaning* (New York: Weatherhill, 1979), p. 152.

p. 44 **Here I would like to be practical:** Ruben L. F. Habito, *Total Liberation* (Maryknoll, NY: Weatherhill, 1970), p. 11.

p. 45 **In this limitless world:** Shunryu Suzuki, *Zen Mind, Beginner's Mind* (Maryknoll, NY: Weatherhill, 1970), p. 29.

p. 46 **Mindfulness and peace are the purpose:** Thich Nhat Hanh, *A Guide to Walking Meditation* (Nyack, NY: Fellowship of Reconciliation, 1985), unpaginated.

p. 73 **In koan work we are given:** John Tarrant Roshi, "Soul in Zen" in *Blind Donkey*, Volume 13, No. 1, June 1992, p. 55.

p. 74 **Probably the simplest definition:** Norman Waddell and Masao Abe, "Shobogenzo Genjokoan," *Eastern Buddhist*, New Series, Volume 5, No. 2, October 1972, p. 130.

p. 76 **After we came out of the church:** James Boswell, *Life of Johnson* (London: Oxford University Press, 1953), p. 333.

p. 81 **Gateless is the Great Tao:** Zenkei Shibayama, *Zen Comments on the Mumonkan* (San Francisco: Harper & Row, 1984), p. 10.

p. 81 **Yamada Roshi used to say:** Robert Aitken, *Gateless Barrier: The Wu-Men Kuan (Mumonkan)* (San Francisco: Northpoint Press, 1990), p. 17.

p. 83 **The priest Tou-shuai set up three barriers:** Robert Aitken, *Gateless Barrier: The Wu-Men Kuan (Mumonkan)* (San Francisco: Northpoint Press, 1990), p. 278.

p. 84 **My advice to you eminent persons:** Isshu Miura and Ruth Fuller Sasaki, *Zen Koan* (New York: Harcourt, Brace & World, 1965), p. 58.

p. 88 **The Priest Tosotsu set up three barriers:** Robert Aitken and Koun Yamada, *Mumonkan* (Honolulu: Diamond Sangha, 1983), pp. 28-29.

p. 91 **So shalt thou feed on death:** William Shakespeare, Sonnet CXLVI.

p. 92 **Yet the problem of death:** Masao Abe, "The Problem of Death," in *The Eastern Buddhist,* Volume XIX, No. 2, Autumn 1986, p. 61.

*Glossary*

**Ancestors**: Those who have gone before. Exemplary teachers and guides on the Great Way.

**Buddha**: (Sanskrit) Literally "awakened one." Generally Gautama Siddhartha, who became the Buddha of history. With Dharma and Sangha, one of the Three Treasures of Buddhism.

**Ch'an**: (Chinese) The Chinese word from which the Japanese word Zen comes. See Zen.

**Chogye**: (Korean) The principal Zen school of Korea. It combines emphasis on koan study (called *Kong-an* in Korean), shikantaza, and some mantric practices. In the West the Kwan Um School of Zen is its principal representative.

**Dharma**: (Sanskrit) Literally "carrying" or "holding." The teachings of the Buddha. The natural order of the universe. The Way. With Buddha and Sangha, one of the Three Treasures of Buddhism.

**Duhkha**: (Pali) Frequently translated as suffering. It signifies the unsatisfactoriness, anxiety, dis-ease characteristic of human existence. The First Noble Truth of the Buddha.

**Eightfold Path**: right view, resolve, speech, conduct, livelihood, effort, mindfulness, and concentration. These are frequently collected together as the three aspects of enlightenment: morality, meditation, and wisdom.

**Four Noble Truths**: 1. Life is characterized by a pervading unsatisfactoriness. 2. This sense of anxiety is caused by clinging to what is passing. 3. One need not suffer in this way. 4. The Eightfold Path of liberation.

**The Great Way**: The way of the Buddha and the ancestors.

**Harada/Yasutani Lineage**: A Japanese lay-led school of Zen derived from the Soto tradition but which incorporates a full koan curriculum in its training. Through such notable figures as Philip Kapleau, Robert Aitken, and Hakuyu Taizan Maezumi, it has been highly influential in the West.

**Jeweled Net of Indra**: An image found in the *Avatamsaka-sutra*. The net extends infinitely in all directions. In each eye is a jewel with infinite facets. The universe exists like that net of jewels, where everything reflects everything else. A metaphor for the phenomenal universe.

**Kensho**: (Japanese) Literally "seeing into reality." Gnosis or wisdom. The experience of awakening in Zen. See also Satori.

**Koan**: (Japanese) Literally a "public case." An object of meditation in Zen training. Largely derived from conversations between Zen students and masters and gathered into collections of "cases."

**Mahayana**: (Sanskrit) Literally the "Great Way." The Buddhism of northern and eastern Asia. Zen is one of the sub-schools of the Mahayana.

**Makyo**: (Japanese) Literally "diabolical manifestation." Hallucinations and visions experienced in Zen meditation.

**Monkey Mind**: A traditional Buddhist expression for the human mind, which is always jumping from one thing to another.

**Nirvana**: (Sanskrit) Literally "extinction." The goal of spiritual practice in Buddhism. The extinction of clinging. The manifestation of wisdom in the phenomenal universe.

**Precepts**: Ethical principles in Buddhism. There are five basic precepts: not killing, lying, stealing, misusing sex, or becoming intoxicated. Also a description of the enlightened mind and action.

**Rinzai**: (Japanese) A school of Japanese Zen emphasizing koan study.

**Samahdi**: (Sanskrit) Literally to "make firm." A state of concentration. A non-dualistic state of awareness.

**Samsara**: (Sanskrit) Literally the "cycle of existence." The transitory world. Traditionally also the cycle of lives.

**Sangha**: (Sanskrit) Literally a "crowd." Traditionally the order of monastics who followed the Buddha. Also all Buddhists. Also the whole of the universe, from buddhas to dust motes. With Buddha and Dharma, one of the Three Treasures of Buddhism.

**Satori**: (Sanskrit) Literally "to know." Gnostic insight of Buddhist awakening. See Kensho.

**Seiza**: (Japanese) Literally "sitting in silence." The traditional Japanese form of sitting, kneeling, and sitting on one's heels.

**Sesshin**: (Japanese) Literally to "touch the mind." A formal Zen retreat of between three and seven days. See Yong Maeng Jong Jin.

**Shikantaza**: (Japanese) Literally "just sitting." Sometimes translated as Silent Illumination or Serene Contemplation. The fundamental practice of Zen meditation. Simple awareness without judgement or discrimination.

**Soto**: (Japanese) A school of Japanese Zen emphasizing the practice of shikantaza.

**Sunyata**: (Sanskrit) Literally "emptiness." Absolute reality.

**Tathagata**: (Sanskrit) Literally the "Thus come one." One who has achieved enlightenment. The Buddha.

**Tanha**: (Pali) Literally "thirst." The clinging consciousness that leads to Duhkha.

**Thien**: (Vietnamese) The Zen school of Vietnam.

**Theravada**: (Pali) Literally the "Way of the Elders." The Buddhism of southeast Asia. Sometimes pejoratively referred to as the Hinayana or Lesser Vehicle.

**Three Treasures**: Buddha, Dharma, and Sangha.

**Vajrayana**: (Sanskrit) Literally the "Diamond vehicle." The school of Buddhism most closely associated with Tibet. Alternate forms also exist in Mongolia, China, and Japan.

**Vipassana**: (Pali) Literally "insight." A type of meditation developed in Theravadan Buddhism similar to shikantaza. Also a contemporary lay-led western school of meditation.

**Wato**: (Japanese) Literally the "word head." The point of resolution in a koan. The wato may be a word such as mu, or a phrase, or the complete text. Many koans have several wato.

**Yong Maeng Jong Jin**: (Korean) Literally "Intrepid Sitting." Also colloquially "To leap like a tiger while sitting." A Zen retreat. See Sesshin.

**Zafu**: (Japanese) Literally a "sitting cushion." A round cushion, usually made of black fabric and stuffed with kapok. Used to sit on in Zen meditation.

**Zazen**: (Japanese) Sitting in Zen meditation. See also Koans and Shikantaza.

**Zen**: (Japanese) From the Sanskrit Dhyana (through the Chinese). Literally absorption or meditation. The principal meditation school of Mahayana Buddhism. Formed in China and strongly influenced by Taoism. In its various expressions Zen extended to Japan, Korea, and Vietnam; and today to most Western countries.

*Resources*

## Books

Masao Abe. *Zen and Western Thought.* Honolulu: University of Hawaii Press, 1985. Abe has generally been acknowledged as the heir to D. T. Suzuki as the scholarly interpreter of Zen Buddism to the West.

Robert Aitken. *Encouraging Words: Zen Buddhist Teachings for Western Students.* New York: Pantheon, 1993. One of Aitken Roshi's many first-rate books, suitable for beginners and old-hands alike.

_____. *The Gateless Barrier: The Wu-Men Kuan (Mumonkan).* San Francisco: Northpoint Press, 1990. The *Wu-men Kuan* is a standard collection of Zen koans. Aitken Roshi translates the text and comments on each of the koans.

_____. *Mind of Clover.* San Francisco: North Point, 1985. A lucid and compassionate study of the moral precepts of Buddhism.

_____. *Taking the Path of Zen*. New York: Farrar, Strauss & Giroux, 1982. The best introduction to Zen Buddhism in the English language by one of the most widely respected Western Zen masters.

Charlotte Joko Beck. *Everyday Zen: Love & Work*. San Francisco: HarperCollins, 1989. A simple, straightforward, and practical volume on daily living by a contemporary Western Zen master.

Thomas Cleary, Translator. *The Original Face: An Anthology of Rinsai Zen*. New York: Weatherhill, 1978. A collection of texts from the Zen school most closely associated with koan study.

_____. *Timeless Spring. A Soto Zen Anthology*. New York: Weatherhill, 1980. A collection of texts from the Zen school most closely associated with the practice of shikantaza, "just sitting."

Francis Cook. *Hua-yen Buddhism: The Jewel Net of Indra*. University Park: Pennsylvania State University, 1977. A good introduction to the Hua-yen literature, the principal philosophical/religious texts associated with the Zen schools.

Fred Eppsteiner, Editor. *The Path of Compassion*. Berkeley: Parallax Press, 1988. Collected essays on the nature of Engaged Buddhism, the evolving western Buddhist expression of social concern. Contributors include the Dalai Lama, Robert Aitken, Thich Nhat Hanh, Joanna Macy, and others.

Rick Fields. *How the Swans Came to the Lake: A Narrative History of Buddhism in America*. Boston: Shambhala, 1986. A very good history, both informative and fun to read.

Frederick Franck, Editor. *The Buddha Eye: An Anthology of the Kyoto School*. New York: Crossroad, 1991. The Kyoto school consists of Japanese philosophers trained in both Western methodologies and the practices of Zen Buddhism. A very good introduction to a fascinating expression of cross-cultural religious and philosophical dialogue.

Rita Gross. *Buddhism After Patriarchy: A Feminist History, Analysis and Reconstruction of Buddhism*. New York: SUNY, 1993. An exciting study presenting some of the wealth of possibilities in the westward movement of Buddhism. Gross is a student of the Vajrayana so, unfortunately, she gives little attention to the Zen traditions. Nonetheless, it is a valuable work.

Ruben Habito. *Healing Breath: Zen Spirituality for a Wounded Earth*. Maryknoll, NY: Orbis, 1993. A wonderful volume by a Christian Zen master that addresses healing within the personal, social, and ecological dimensions of life.

Philip Kapleau. *The Three Pillars of Zen: Teaching, Practice, Enlightenment*. Boston: Beacon, 1967. One of the first authentic introductions to Zen in English. Of particular interest because of the kensho descriptions in Part Two.

John Daido Loori. *The Eight Gates of Zen*. Mt. Tremper, NY: Dharma Communications, 1992. A first rate overview of Zen Buddhism by one of this country's premier Zen masters. It also contains a lucid argument for the development of a Western Buddhist monasticism.

Joanna Macy. *World as Lover, World as Self*. Berkeley: Parallax, 1991. A collection of essays by one of the foremost thinkers on Engaged Buddhism. Macy has served on the faculty of Starr

King School for a number of years and is particularly accessible for Unitarian Universalists.

Isshu Miura and Ruth Fuller Sasaki. *Zen Koan.* New York: Harcourt, Brace & World, 1965. The only competent introduction to the Zen koan in the English language.

Wong Mou-lam, Translator. *The Sutra of Wei Lang (Hui Neng).* Boston: Shambhala, 1990. The earliest English translation of this delightful Zen classic remains a very good version.

Thich Nhat Hanh. *Being Peace.* Berkeley: Parallax Press, 1987. A good introduction to the writings of the Vietnamese Zen master, poet, and peace activist.

Keiji Nishitani. *Religion and Nothingness.* Berkeley: University of California Press, 1982. A genuine classic in the philosophical investigation of Zen Buddhism.

Walpola Rahula. *What the Buddha Taught.* New York: Grove Press, 1974. A classic of the emerging western Buddhism. A clean and concise introduction to the fundamentals of Buddhist teachings by a Theravadan monk and scholar.

Seung Sahn. *Only Don't Know: The Teaching Letters of Zen Master Seung Sahn.* San Francisco: Four Seasons Foundation, 1982. A very good introduction to the teaching style of the great Korean Zen missionary to the West.

H.W. Schumann. *The Historical Buddha.* London: Arkana, 1989. A "form critical" of the Buddha's life. Comprehensive and persuasive.

*The Shambhala Dictionary of Buddhism and Zen.* Boston: Shambhala, 1991. The standard dictionary.

Ellen Sidor, Editor. *A Gathering of Spirit: Women Teachers in American Buddhism.* Cumberland: Primary Point, 1987. Essays by Western women Buddhist teachers, including Zen masters Maurine Stuart, Gesshin Prabhasa, Barbara Rhodes, and Jan Chozen Bays.

John Snelling. *The Buddhist Handbook: A Complete Guide to Buddhist Schools, Teaching, Practice and History.* Rochester: Inner Traditions, 1991. A good overview of contemporary Buddhism. Of particular interest is "Who's Who in Buddhism," listing many important contemporary teachers.

D. T. Suzuki. *Manual of Zen Buddhism.* New York: Grove Press, 1960. A classic that remains a very good source for fundamental Mahayana and Zen texts.

Shunryu Suzuki. *Zen Mind, Beginner's Mind.* New York: Weatherhill, 1970. Consists of Dharma talks by one of the first Japanese Zen missionaries to the West. A graceful exposition of the Way.

Kazuaki Tanahashi, Editor. *Moon in a Dewdrop: Writings of Zen Master Dogen.* San Francisco: Northpoint, 1985. A collection of the writings of a Zen teacher considered one of the finest minds and greatest spiritual directors in medieval Japan.

Robert Thurman, Translator. *The Holy Teachings of Vimalakirti: A Mahayana Scripture.* University Park: Pennsylvania State University, 1976. A classic Buddhist text recounting the teachings of the enlightened lay-person Vimalakirti.

M. H. Trevor, Translator. *The Ox and His Herdsman.* Tokyo: Hokuseido Press, 1969. A map of "Zen enlightenment."

Burton Watson, Translator. *The Zen Teachings of Master Lin-chi*. Boston: Shambhala, 1993. The teachings of the great ninth-century Chinese master of the koan way. A classic of Zen literature.

## Periodicals

*Tricycle: The Buddhist Review*, 163 West 22nd St., New York, NY 100111. Phone (212) 645-1143, FAX (212) 645-1493. Email tricycle@echonyc.com.

*Turning Wheel: Journal of the Buddhist Peace Fellowship,* PO Box 4650, Berkeley, CA 94704. Phone (510) 525-8596.

*UU Sangha: Newsletter of the Unitarian Universalist Buddhist Fellowship,* c/o the Reverend Samuel Trumbore, First Unitarian Universalist Society in Albany, 405 Washington Avenue, Albany, NY 12206.